GUILT-FREE SELF-CARE

It's easier than you think!

EMMA FEAR

Dedicated to Sophie & Joshua

TABLE OF CONTENTS

Introduction

"*An empty lantern provides no light. Self-care is the fuel that allows your light to shine brightly.*"
Unknown

Why I wrote this book

In the last few years, self-care has become a hot topic. And whilst I know it can only be a good thing, I have always struggled to practise it. I'm the type of person who always has to be doing something. I struggle to sit down and just read my book on a weekend, feeling like I have to earn it by doing the housework first or waiting for the permission that being on holiday provides. As much as I can see the benefits of self-care, there always seems to be something more important to do or think about. So why is it so hard to do? And why exactly should we be doing it?

That's what I wanted to answer by writing this book. I wanted to dig deep into why we should be practising self-care in a bid to give myself, and you, permission to do so. To dispel the belief that it is in some way selfish or lazy. And then look at ways in which we can build self-care into our lives, especially if, like me, you are a working mum. If, like me, you already struggle to fit everything you need to (or think you need to fit) into the day or week, without adding "practise self-care" to your never-ending to-do list, then this book is for you. If, like me, you feel guilty enough about sometimes putting work before your children and the thought of then putting yourself before them too is just a step too far, then this book is for you. If you're not convinced you would actually put your oxygen mask on before your child's if ever you were in the unfortunate position of having to do so, then this book is for you.

When collating my list of 40 ways to practise self-care, I also explored the "why" for each of the activities or changes in behaviour I included. This really helped me to justify not only their inclusion in this book but also in my everyday life. Like many, I am time-poor, so I need a good reason as to why I should be spending my time on something – even if it is something so clearly important. (Admittedly, I am also guilty of wasting my precious time scrolling on social media without any justification whatsoever!) Adding the "why" though is so important when trying to change behaviour, because it tells our brain why it should be paying attention. I have also focused on ensuring that the activities or behaviours included in this book are things that can easily be integrated into our already maxed-out lives and suggested practical ways to implement them. The issue I have with a lot of books of this nature is that they are very good at explaining the "why" but fall down on the "how".

Writing this book has helped me to recognise when I am not practising what, some might say, I am trying to preach. Halfway through writing this book, I had a mini meltdown on a Zoom call with a friend, getting myself completely worked up about something that had happened work. I was in pure overthinking mode and feeling completely overwhelmed by everything that was going on. My friend, who knew I was writing this book, asked me whether I had done any of the things I was writing about recently. The answer was no. I was so focused on everything else, I totally forgot to think about myself. I spent the rest of the day sat on the sofa reading a book, followed by a long soak in a bubble bath and having a family take-away. The next day things didn't seem nearly half as bad. Taking that time out gave me some perspective. So now, as soon as I feel that feeling of overwhelm starting to creep back in, I make myself do one of the activities mentioned in this book and it stops that overwhelm in its tracks.

How to use this book

Okay, so here is the big confession. I do not follow all 40 self-care practices set out in this book. I would love to say I do, but I don't. However, I have tried them all at one time or another and a lot of them I do practice reasonably regularly. And some others more sporadically. The main thing though is that I recognise the importance of incorporating at least some of these practices into my life. And feel so much better when I do.

So, at the risk of making you think I am trying to short-change you, please don't try and do everything listed in the following pages as soon as you finish reading them. In fact, don't feel like you have to try all of them at all. You'll just put way too much pressure on yourself and feel even worse than before you picked up this book (clearly something neither of us wants!) All I ask is that you give some of them a go. And just see what works for you. You can choose to read through the whole book in order and then decide which ones you want to have a go at. Or you can check out the table of contents and focus on those you are drawn to. You might want to pick two or three to start with and then add in more.

Some are daily habits to try and build in, others are less frequent. And some are really easy to do, others take more time. I would though recommend starting with Chapter 1, "Ditch the guilt", which is a barrier many of us need to overcome before we can start moving self-care up the priority scale.

So, grab yourself your beverage of choice, find a quiet spot where you are least likely to be ambushed by a child/partner/animal/Amazon delivery driver and enjoy!

Emma x

Chapter 1
Ditch the guilt

"Guilt is the thief of life." Anthony Hopkins

The Why

One of the biggest barriers to practising self-care is the guilt we feel when we put ourselves first. This is often more pronounced in women than it is in men and even more so in mothers. There often feels like there is something we "should" be doing rather than the self-care activity we "want" to be doing. Or, perhaps just as often, we "want" to be doing something for someone else when we "should" be doing a self-care activity. We feel guilty for wanting to do something for ourselves rather than spending time with our children. We feel guilty if we sit down and read our book for half an hour when there is a pile of laundry that needs folding and putting away. We feel the need to justify to others why we have sat down, *"I've been running around all day so just need five minutes to sit down, which I never do by the way..."* Or we turn self-care into a reward, something we have to earn as a way to avoid the guilt – once I have put away the laundry then I can read my book or I'll just run the hoover round the lounge and then I can treat myself to five minutes sat down with a cup of tea. Or I can only watch that new episode of my latest Netflix series if I do so while doing the ironing. There is of course nothing wrong with combining the ironing with something you enjoy – in fact it is to be recommended! However, there is equally nothing wrong with just doing something you enjoy and nothing else and it is also to be recommended.

As stated in the introduction to this book, self-care is critical for our wellbeing and mental health. It should be up there with eating healthily and doing enough exercise. Do you feel guilty about skipping dessert or going to the gym? Probably quite the opposite in fact! (Or you go to the gym to earn your dessert!) So, you shouldn't feel guilty about taking some time out for you.

The How

But how do you stop feeling guilty about practising self-care?

Recognise the importance of self-care

Hopefully reading this book will help you with this and, the fact that you have bought this book demonstrates that you do at least acknowledge that self-care has some value, or are actually taking the time to read it, if it was a gift. As mentioned throughout these pages, self-care can help boost your physical and mental health, avoid burnout and reduce stress. It is an essential part of looking after ourselves and should not be viewed as a "nice-to-have".

Reframe your view of what self-care actually is

A lot of us translate "self-care" into "self-indulgence", which makes us feel guilty for even thinking about it. But that's not what it is. It is not about making yourself feel good or indulging yourself; it is about maintaining, and improving, your physical and mental wellbeing. The fact it will also make you feel good is an added bonus. And it doesn't have to be extravagant or indulgent, it can be as simple as you like, even just taking 10 minutes to sit quietly and watch the world go by. That's not to say that on occasion it shouldn't be self-indulgent, and in fact some of the suggested activities in this book could be classed as such. There is absolutely nothing wrong with a bit of self-indulgence every now and then!

Give yourself permission

This is a simple but effective. Just say to yourself that you give yourself permission to take some time out for you to focus on your needs. And that you will be a better person/mother/wife/partner if you do. Repeat this as often as you need to in order to start believing it.

Acknowledge the resentment

Have you ever found yourself starting to feel resentful of your partner, your children or your colleagues? When you are having to constantly put their needs before your own? It may sound harsh and uncomfortable to acknowledge that but it is important that you do because that resentment can build up and become a source of stress in your relationships. View self-care as a form of resilience-building. Taking the time to focus on your needs as well as the needs of others will prevent that resentment from building. Recognising this fact means you can view self-care as a form of preventative medicine for your relationships.

Think about the message you are sending your children

This is particularly important if you have a daughter. Children learn from their parents and develop their beliefs at a young age based on the behaviour of their parents. Think back to your childhood and your mum's behaviour and attitude around self-care. Was it something you saw her practising? Or do you get the sense she spent all her energy on looking after other people? Do you ever feel like you sound like your mother talking when you are justifying spending any time or money on yourself? Chances are that, if you witnessed this behaviour in your childhood, you are modelling those same behaviours yourself, albeit subconsciously.

Think about how your behaviour has the potential to impact your children. If all your daughter sees is you running around after everyone else, exhausted and exasperated and seemingly never doing something for yourself, what message is that sending her? If she hears you justifying why you are taking some time out to read your book or why you have locked the bathroom door, what message is that sending her? And if you have a son, what is he learning to expect from any future females in his life?

Rather ironically, if you can't practise self-care for yourself without feeling guilty, practise it for the sake of your children.

Stop viewing "doing nothing" as a dirty word (well, two dirty words, to be precise!)

We have long associated doing nothing with laziness and other negative connotations, with phrases such as "the devil makes work for idle hands" promoting this view. And yes, doing nothing all the time should be discouraged. However, there is absolutely nothing wrong with doing nothing some of the time, quite the opposite in fact. Taking time out to stop and do nothing has many benefits, many of which are covered elsewhere in this book. Sitting down without any distractions gives the mind time to properly think and allows the subconscious mind to come to the fore. This can lead to increased creativity, better self-awareness and reduced stress. So instead of viewing "doing nothing" as something to avoid, flip your thinking to view it as "doing something" to enhance your wellbeing. Now keep on reading this book through a guilt-free lense!

The Short Version

- Do not feel like you have to justify or earn your self-care activities.
- Recognise the important role of self-care in helping to boost your physical and mental health, avoid burnout and reduce stress.
- Reframe your view of what self-care actually is – it is not a form of indulgence or extravagance; it is a necessity.
- Give yourself permission to take some time to focus on your needs.
- Recognise that you will be a better person/mother/wife/partner through the practice of self-care.
- Acknowledge any resentment you may feel towards your partner or children if you always put their needs before yours and overcome that resentment through self-care.
- If you can't do it for you, do it for your children by focusing on the example you are setting them.
- Stop viewing "doing nothing" as a dirty word (or two)!

Chapter 2
Boundaries

"You are not required to set yourself on fire to keep others warm." Unknown

The Why

Have you ever felt like you're being pulled in all directions? Or find yourself doing something for someone else and slightly (or even greatly) resenting having to do so? Or get to the end of the workday and find it hard to actually walk away from your to do list – there is always just one more thing on your list you want to get done. Or find yourself, when working from home, starting earlier and earlier? Then you may need to look at your boundaries and learn how to set them, as well as respect them.

Boundaries are a key aspect of self-care, if not *the* key aspect, because boundaries are all about respecting yourself and your time and ensuring your needs are met, and not encroached upon, before looking after the needs of others. And I think women in particular find it difficult to set boundaries and ensure they, and others, respect them. We've seen generations of women before us live their lives with no such boundaries. Putting the needs of their husbands and then children and then parents first. Without wishing to be too stereotypical, a lot of us grew up watching our mothers live their lives around the needs of others – timing dinner around their husband's arrival home, always running around doing housework, looking after children, ferrying children, shopping, cleaning and so on. Only once they had done everything they "needed" to do done would they then allow themselves the "luxury" of sitting down in the evening to watch Coronation Street. There are of course exceptions to this view but an element of this is engrained into many of our psyches. And whilst there is absolutely nothing wrong if a woman wants to assume this more traditional role in the family, it is a concern if they still do this without setting any boundaries. This may be why a lot of women find this issue with boundaries spills into their work life too. Add into the mix those of us who are natural people pleasers then boundaries become even more challenging!

But what do I mean when I talk about boundaries?

Well, there are several types of boundaries – physical, mental, personal, professional… The main boundary I am talking about though is the one around time – more specifically, your time. This means recognising that your time is precious and that you should spend it doing the things that are important to you and what makes you happy. This doesn't necessarily mean you get to spend all your time doing what you want to do. There are always going be things that we have to do that we might prefer not to, such as changing that stinky nappy, taking the kids to their various sports clubs or putting in a few extra hours at work to meet that deadline. What it does mean though is that it should be on our own terms.

The How

There are two sides to boundaries, the first is setting them and the second is sticking to them. To set boundaries, first you need to identify where they are missing. Think through your last week. When did you feel resentful of doing something? What things did you do that drained your energy? When did you feel that you just didn't have a moment to catch your breath? Did you start and finish work at your contracted times? Did you take a full lunchbreak? What have you been wanting to do all week but just haven't been able to get round to it? These are all good indicators of where you may be lacking boundaries or you have boundaries but are not sticking to them.

If your boundaries around your work time versus personal time are non-existent or weak, make the decision that you will not start work until a set time each day and make sure you finish your workday on a set time each day. This doesn't necessarily have to be your contracted start and finish time – you could take the view that you need that extra half an hour head start in the morning to get a jump on the day before everyone else gets online. And that's fine, provided you are comfortable in that decision. If you find yourself constantly checking your emails in the evenings and weekends, take the decision not to do that. Or, if that is too much of a leap, allot a specific time each evening and at the weekends when you will check them and don't check them outside of those times.

If you are lacking boundaries around some "you-time", decide how much time you would like to (or even need to) dedicate to yourself each day, or each week. And then schedule it in. Add it to your calendar and the family calendar. You can simply block out time and leave it at that or you could list out all the things you want to do, such as go for a walk or run, go to an exercise class, draw, read, learn a musical instrument, watch your current Netflix series-of-choice or phone a friend. Then schedule when you want to do your chosen activity.

Having a planned activity can sometimes make it easier to uphold those boundaries but your boundary is no less important if you don't have a specific activity planned – sometimes you just need to have some time to stop and think or to have the freedom to be spontaneous (and yes, I see the irony of scheduling time to be spontaneous!) Make sure you have childcare in place, if relevant, and ensure your other half (again, if relevant) has the appointment in their calendar too. This may seem like overkill but it is really important to remove as many potential reasons why your boundaries will be breached.

And this leads onto the second element of boundaries – sticking to them. Setting them is actually pretty easy to do. It is protecting them that is often the challenge. And there's lots of reasons why this might be. On the work-front, it can be so tempting to "just finish this email", which then leads to another piece of work, which of course takes longer than you thought and before you know it you are half an hour past the finish time you agreed with yourself. Or if you don't have something specific to move onto when you finish work, like needing to pick up children or get to an exercise class, you might not see the harm in doing an extra half an hour or so. The harm though is that you don't get to switch off from work and there is always something else you could be doing, like talking to your children about their day, going for a walk or getting a head start on dinner.

On the personal-front, a big barrier to sticking to your boundaries may be that you don't actually consider time spent on you as being important. The needs of others always seem more important and you can always go to your class next week. Or you may feel guilty for taking some time out for you and so actually welcome the excuse of needing to take your daughter to her friend's house as a way to avoid that feeling of guilt. But what are you teaching your daughter by missing your favourite class? That if she becomes a mum that her time is no longer as precious as others? Don't get me wrong, I'm not saying that you should always put your needs ahead of your children's – that's equally not something I'd want my daughter to grow-up thinking. What I am saying though, using the same example, is that you shouldn't automatically drop your class to play taxi driver. When you picked your class, you would have chosen a time when there were no other family commitments scheduled and put it on your calendar. So, your daughter could either arrange another day to go out or wait until your class has finished. And one question I would ask in that scenario is if you had a work meeting scheduled rather than your exercise or art class, would you miss that meeting to take your daughter to her friend's house? I'm guessing not, so why would you cancel an appointment with yourself?

So how do you make sure you uphold your boundaries? As mentioned above, you treat them with respect. As also mentioned above, you let others know about them – you put them in your work and personal calendars and add to the family calendar (I've even been known to send my husband an Outlook appointment so he has no excuse not to remember I'm out!) You set expectations with your work colleagues and your family. You let work colleagues know you won't be responding to emails in the evenings or at weekends and, if your role means that you do need to be available in an emergency, ask them to call or text you if it really cannot wait until normal working hours. You can even set up rules for your inbox so you only get email notifications from certain people. You tell your family that you won't be available at the times specified and that they are only to disturb you in the case of an emergency (and wi-fi going off is not an emergency). And if the thought of doing all this is scary, rest assured it does get easier as people's expectations about your availability and willingness to sacrifice your time change. Your boss may be a little taken aback the first time you don't respond to a non-urgent email sent Friday evening until Monday morning but once they realise you are not going to respond to emails outside working hours it will become the norm again (if it doesn't then perhaps you need to reassess whether that's the type of work culture you want to continue to work in). And your daughter may throw the biggest strop that she can't go to her friend's house but will hopefully learn to check the family calendar before making arrangements next time.

I will be honest though, not letting your boundaries get encroached, either by yourself or others, is hard to maintain. It is so easy to slip back into old habits and if you do, don't give up – just reset expectations again – both yours, and others' – and redraw your boundaries. And there will be exceptions you will have to make. Times when that piece of work really cannot wait until the morning or when your childcare arrangements fall through or your child just really needs you. Those exceptions are absolutely fine and, you will find, not something you resent as you may do now, because you know that they are genuine exceptions and no longer the rule.

The Short Version

- Your time is precious and setting boundaries around your time helps to protect your personal time.
- Decide what you want your time boundaries around work and family commitments to be and communicate those boundaries to others.
- Treat scheduled personal time with the same respect you would a work or family commitment.
- It will take time to adjust to having stronger boundaries but persevere and you will feel the benefit.
- There will be times when your boundaries do get encroached but ensure it is on your terms and is the exception rather than the rule.

Chapter 3
Buy yourself some flowers

"Flowers are like friends; They bring colour to your world." Leonardo Da Vinci

The Why

I love having fresh flowers in the house and as I sit here writing I have a vase of tulips beside me, which I bought myself at the weekend. For years though I would rely on my husband to bring me flowers, so we very rarely had flowers in the house! It felt far too extravagant to spend £5 on some flowers. But then I realised it was all about priorities. If I could spend my money on a bottle of wine or buying my lunch rather than making it, then I could afford to buy some flowers occasionally. The added bonus being that the flowers make me happy and that feeling can last all week (if I remember to top up their water!) – unlike a bottle of wine which lasts an evening and definitely does not make me feel very happy the morning after.

And there is some science to back up my attributing happiness to having flowers in the house. A study by the Complementary Therapies in Medicine gave college-aged women a vase of roses for their dorm rooms and these were shown to help them feel more relaxed and stress-free. Another study, from Harvard University Medical School, by Dr. Nancy Etcoff, found that having flowers in the home led to participants feeling more compassion towards others, having less worry and anxiety, and feeling less depressed.

The How

The easiest way is of course to buy yourself some! Instead of walking past the flowers section in the supermarket next time you are there, stop and choose a bunch and add to your trolley. Having said that, the even easier way, but admittedly quite a bit more expensive, is to subscribe to a flower delivery service, such as Bloom & Wild or Freddies Flowers. You'll be sent fresh flowers each month and all that is left to do is follow their instructions on how to arrange them in the vessel of your choice. The great thing about a subscription service is that it's often a nice surprise when they arrive.

But if you would prefer to buy your own flowers, which

ones should you buy? The quick answer is any that you find appealing. If you want to get more intentional about the type of flowers then here are few that come with some added benefits.

Roses
A classic choice but a good one. Roses have been shown to help reduce stress and promote relaxation. Red roses are said to boost physical energy, confidence and courage, as well as promoting alertness, so an even better choice if you are feeling tired. If you are looking for a calming effect though, opt for pink roses, the colour pink having been shown to also promote relaxation, so a double whammy of calmness!

Chrysanthemums
Chrysanthemums are said to help reduce feelings of worry and stress, so a good option for when you have something on your mind. And if you opt for yellow ones, you have the added bonus of the colour yellow inspiring happiness and confidence – great for when you're facing a new challenge.

Gerbera Daisy
A study by NASA found that Gerbera Daisies are great at removing benzene found in solvents, paints, gas and detergents. So not only do they look pretty, but they also help keep your air clean.

Tulips

As these are my favourite, I couldn't not include them! The great thing about tulips is the wide variety of colours they can come in, meaning you can create a beautiful arrangement that will brighten up your day. They are also said to represent perfect love and so it is suggested you should give them to someone you have deep, conditional love for – so who better to give them to than yourself!

If you can't afford to buy flowers (and I mean *really* can't afford – see above point on priorities) then take a look in your garden, if you have one, to see if there are any flowers in there you could bring indoors. Even a jam jar full of dandelions can brighten up your room. Or if you would prefer not to have the regular expense of buying cut flowers, look for colourful pot plants to add to your home, such as a Poinsettia, African Violets or Orchids. And if the thought of having to try and keep something else alive other than you and your kids makes you want to cry, you can get some gorgeous artificial blooms nowadays that look extremely realistic – so no maintenance at all, not even adding them to water!

The Short Version

- Not only does having flowers in your house brighten up your home, it's proven to promote feelings of calm and to reduce depression.

- Opt for a subscription service, such as Bloom & Wild or Freddies Flowers, or simply pick up a bunch next time you are passing a flower shop or doing your weekly shop in the supermarket.

- Choose whichever flowers appeal to you at the time or get intentional by choosing flowers for a specific purpose, such as red roses to boost energy and confidence.

- And if you can't afford to buy flowers, take a look in your garden or local park – even a jam jar full of dandelions or daisies can bring great joy.

Chapter 4
Have a bath

"There must be quite a few things that a hot bath won't cure, but I don't know many of them."
Sylvia Plath

The Why

After a long day, there is nothing I like more than a soak in a hot bath – preferably with some posh bath oil or bubble bath. Often, I'll listen to a podcast or read my book and, if it's a Friday night, might even have a glass of something on the side. If I'm feeling really fancy, I'll even light a candle! I am guilty of having my baths nuclear hot, which means I don't always last in them as long as I would like to. But I do always feel better afterwards. Often, I will have one after I've finished work on a Friday as it signals that the work week is done and it's time to slow it all down and turn on weekend mode.

So, I would 100% recommend taking the time to chill out (or, if you're like me, slowly cook like boil in the bag rice) in a bath at least once a week. And make sure you lock the door – the aforementioned candle, despite its strong scent, was not enough to mask my ten-year-old son's interruption to my bath the other day!

But for those of you who don't want to just take my word for it, I've done some research into the benefits of a bath to help persuade you to take the plunge more often, and set out my findings below.

It burns calories

Yes, apparently, soaking in a hot bath can actually burn calories. A study[1], led by Steve Faulkner at Loughborough University, involved 14 "habitually inactive" participants (apparently doing less than 1.5 hours of structured physical activity in a week gains you the badge of "habitually inactive") spending either 60 minutes sat in a hot bath or 60 minutes cycling. The water temperature was set at 40°c – enough to raise your body temperature by 1°c in an hour. And although the participants enduring the hour's cycling did burn more calories than those sat in the bath (no surprises there!), those enjoying a soak burned around 140 calories – the

1   "The effect of passive heating on heat shock protein 70 and interleukin-6: A possible treatment tool for metabolic diseases?", S. H. Faulkner, S. Jackson, G. Fatania & C. A. Leicht (2017)

equivalent to spending 30 minutes walking[2]. The study did point out that exercise brings with it several other benefits so this isn't a reason to skip your weekly online fitness class if favour of the bathtub. It does though provide another good reason to make time for a little you time in the bath.

It can help improve your mental health

Various studies have shown that regular hot baths can help improve mental wellbeing. For example, one study, reported in the NewScientist[3], found that long soaks in a hot bath twice a week could help with depression, thought to be down to the effect raising our body temperature has on our circadian rhythms. Circadian rhythms regulate our sleep patterns and are often seen to be erratic or off-kilter in those with depression. After eight weeks of spending 30 minutes in a hot bath (again, 40°C) for up to 30 minutes, followed by 20 minutes wrapped up in blankets with hot water bottles, the participants scored lower on a depression scale. And the benefits were seen as early as two weeks after the study started. Again, it seems important that the bath raises our body temperature, so it does need to be a hot bath.

2   "A hot bath has benefits similar to exercise", 20 March 2017, Steve Faulkner, The Conversation

3   "Hot baths could improve depression as much as physical exercise", 22 March 2018, Claire Wilson, NewScientist

Another study compared the effects of showering compared to having a bath and found that a bath appeared to be more beneficial to mental and physical health than showering[4].

It helps alleviate stress

Submerging yourself in a warm bath can help calm anxiety and relieve stress. In fact, there is a whole therapy dedicated to the benefit of water – hydrotherapy. And whilst cold water hydrotherapy focuses on stimulation, the warm water variety can be used to soothe the mind. To enhance the benefits of the warm water, calming essential oils, such as lavender, rose and bergamot, can be added.

It helps relieve aching muscles

Being hunched over a desk or on your feet all day can result in various aches and pains or muscle stiffness. A warm bath gets your blood moving, which helps relieve sore muscles and loosen tight ones. Adding Epsom salts can help further with this, shown to reduce inflammation, thanks to their high magnesium content.

---

4 "Physical and Mental Effects of Bathing: A Randomized Intervention Study", Goto Y, Hayasaka S, Kurihara S, Nakamura Y, 7 June 2018

The How

I won't insult your intelligence by telling you how to run a bath! My top tips though are to pick a time when you are less likely to be disturbed, light a few candles, put on some music and lock the door!

What I will do though is make a few suggestions as to what to add to your bath to make it that extra bit special and what to actually do in your bath!

What to add to your bath

As well as the aforementioned bath salts, there are lots of things you can use to make your bath even more relaxing or to provide other benefits, such as relieving dry skin. Here are a few options to think about.

Essential oils

Essential oils have some fantastic properties that you can benefit from by adding them to your bath. Not only do they add a nice scent, many of them assist with relaxation and can help relieve various ailments. For relaxation, try soothing chamomile, calming rose and geranium or relaxing lavender. If you're looking for a more uplifting soak, opt for energising peppermint and rosemary or invigorating black pepper and tea tree. And if you need to soothe aching muscles, try warming eucalyptus combined with lavender, rosemary or chamomile.

To add them to your bath, you should first mix them with another oil, such as sunflower oil, which will help the oil disperse in the water, as well as soften the skin. Simply mix together 4-5 drops of your essential oil(s) with a tablespoon of the sunflower oil and then add to your bath once it has been run. You can also use full-fat milk instead of the sunflower oil.

Alternatively, you can make it even easier for yourself and buy some ready-made bath oil with essential oils – Neal's Yard do some lovely ones.

Bath salts

As already mentioned, Epsom salts are good for relieving inflammation and so a good option after exercise. Bath salts in general though are also good for other reasons. It is believed that the minerals in the salts, including magnesium, sodium chloride and potassium, can be absorbed through the skin, although further research is needed in this area. This boosts your mineral levels, restores your body and can also relax the nervous system.

Oats

Yes, I really am suggesting putting oats in your bath! Not directly, as that would just be unpleasant, but wrapped in a small piece of muslin or a pair of old tights. Alternatively, grind the oats in a food blender until fine enough to dissolve in the water and then add a couple of handfuls to your bath. Oat baths can be used to treat a variety of skin conditions, including eczema, psoriasis and sunburn, as well as dry skin in general, thanks to their anti-inflammatory and moisturising properties.

Bicarbonate of soda

Adding bicarbonate, or baking soda as it also known, has similar benefits as oats in terms of helping treat skin conditions, with its natural exfoliating, anti-inflammatory and anti-fungal properties. It is particularly good if you are fighting a yeast infection or fungal nail or skin condition. Simply add two cups of baking soda to your bath or combine with Epsom salts and your choice of essential oil for the ultimate stress-relieving, muscle-soothing, skin-healing and relaxing bath time!

What to do in your bath

This may sound like a statement of the obvious but bear with me. As I mentioned above, I often like to read or listen to a podcast. I know of others who like to listen to music or a meditation. The point is that what I am not doing is lying there worrying about everything that is going on in my life, the things I think I "should" be doing rather than lying in the bath or stressing about my never-ending to-do list. What I am doing, and what you should be doing in your bath too, is relaxing. For me, that is reading my book and it might be for you too.

Or you might want to watch an episode of your latest Netflix binge-watch or listen to some chilled music. You may even want to try doing nothing and just enjoying some quiet time or practising some mindfulness (see chapter 36). The main thing is that you switch off from the daily stresses and worries and relax.

The Short Version

- As well as being a relaxing pastime, having a warm bath has a number of health benefits. These include burning calories, improving your mental health, alleviating stress and relieving aching muscles.
- Try adding essential oils, bath salts, oats or bicarbonate of soda to give your bath some extra oomph.
- Listen to music or a podcast, read a book or watch Netflix if you are in danger of lying there worrying about whatever is on your mind.

Chapter 5
Nice shower gel

"Shower the people you love with love." James Taylor

The Why

This is a simple one but a little indulgence that makes me smile in the morning. For years I opted for whatever shower gel was on offer and didn't think too much about what I was using in the shower beyond that. But then one Christmas my husband bought me some fancy shower gel and I was hooked. It was so much thicker than the usual stuff I bought so felt much more luxurious, and it smelt amazing. The smell also lingered way beyond when I stepped out of the shower.

What it also made me do was to stop the usual myriad of thoughts going through my head whilst in the shower and focus for a moment on how good it smelt. So effectively, a form of mindfulness (see chapter 36 for why this is so important).

And I love it even more now that I buy it for myself. Before, I wouldn't have dreamt of spending more than £1.99 on shower gel because it felt like an unnecessary extravagance. But part of practising self-care is recognising your own self-worth and treating yourself as you would your best friend. Would I give my best friend the shower gel I was buying for myself before? Nope! But I would the one I buy now.

The How

Next time you are running low on shower gel, take the opportunity to upgrade. There are plenty out there to choose from and it doesn't have to be expensive. Taking the time to select one that contains natural ingredients and is free from the likes of parabens and sodium lauryl sulphates is also a good way to practise self-care. By doing so, you are acknowledging that you are worth spending that extra time doing a little research and reading the labels. Look out for scents that appeal to you, perhaps opting for an uplifting citrus based one for the morning and a more calming lavender or floral based one in the evening. And yes, you can buy two different ones! Variety is the spice of life and mixing up your scents will help keep them fresh.

Once you have your nice new shower gel, use it as a reason to practise some mindfulness in the shower each morning. I cover mindfulness in more detail in chapter 36 but, in essence, it just means simply being present in your shower. You can do this by focusing on how the shower gel looks and smells as you squeeze some onto your hand. How thick is it? What colour is it? And then how it feels when you wash yourself with it. Breathe in the scent and pay attention to each part of your body as you wash yourself. Feel the water rush over you as you rinse yourself off, feel its warmth and take some deep breaths. Just spending five minutes focusing on the task at hand in the shower, rather than running through the hamster wheel of thoughts you usually do, is a great way to start the day on the right foot or to end it on the right note.

The Short Version

- Upgrade your shower gel.
- Opt for a more natural shower gel that doesn't contain parabens and sodium lauryl sulphates.
- Focus on the smell and feel of your shower gel when using it, as a form of mindfulness.

Chapter 6
Have a beauty treatment

"Because you're worth it." L'Oréal

The Why

Several people, when asked what self-care is, will respond by naming some sort of beauty treatment, such as having their nails done or getting a facial. And yes, this is a form of self-care (why else would I be including it!) However, what is important to note is that it is only self-care if you are doing it for yourself. There is a difference between going to the salon because it makes you feel good and going there to keep yourself looking good for other people – be that your partner, your friends or your social media followers. And with the rise in popularity of Botox, fillers and other youth-boosting procedures, it is important to question your motives when considering any of these treatments. Are you trying to make yourself look younger because it makes you feel good or because you are worried about what others think? If the latter is true then try and spend some time thinking about why you are worried about this and looking at other ways to overcome this worry.

At the other extreme are those who view a trip to the beauty salon as extravagant and something reserved for the self-obsessed social media stars and footballers' wives. This view also needs to be challenged. If you feel like this then question why exactly. Is it because you don't think getting a facial or your nails done is something you would enjoy? Or do you think you would enjoy it and are slightly envious when you see friends' polished fingertips but view such treatments as a waste of money? If so, delve a bit deeper into why you think this. Is it because you don't think you are worth spending that money on? If it is then perhaps it's time to re-evaluate the view you have of yourself and recognise that you are worthy of all the money in the world. Maybe you believe taking care of your appearance is a sign of vanity and getting a beauty treatment is something only self-obsessed people do. If this is how you feel then have a think about what caused you to think like this. Is this something that stems from childhood? Perhaps you were told as a child to stop looking in the mirror so much or not to spend so long in the bathroom. Or do you view taking care of your appearance as a waste of time or not worth the effort? If so, question why you don't care (or no longer care) what you look like. This can be a sign of depression and if you can't work out the answer yourself or how to change that mindset then consider seeking professional help.

As you can see, your attitude to beauty treatments can reveal quite a lot about your attitude to self-care and how you value yourself. Where you want to get to is viewing beauty treatments as something that you do for you because they make you feel good and, in the words of L'Oréal, because you are worth it.

And whilst you can do your own nails, have an at-home facial and pluck your own eyebrows, treating yourself to having any, or all of these, done professionally will usually (at least in my case) lead to a much better result! I have never mastered the art of painting my nails (and just my nails, not the surrounding fingertips) and I usually combine a face mask with a stupidly hot bath meaning the face mask slides off my face within two minutes! So having these done professionally is not only a great treat that makes me feel good about myself, it also means they are done properly!

The How

If you're not quite ready to commit to regular visits to the salon, start off with the occasional treat. It has become a holiday ritual of mine to get my nails done before going away (or in the airport if I run out of time!) and my daughter and I started a Christmas Eve tradition a few years ago of going to get our nails done together. You could also treat yourself for your birthday or to celebrate reaching a work or fitness goal. Or, even better, just because!

If you're not sure what you should get done, have a read through the treatments on offer and see what jumps out. And if some of the prices put you off, start with the less expensive treatments, such as an eyebrow shape or lash tint. I am no beauty treatment connoisseur but both of these treatments have a significant impact on how I look and feel and, the lash tint in particular, are not things I can do very well myself. In terms of which salon to go to, ask friends for recommendations or read reviews on Facebook or Google.

If you're concerned about the cost, not because you don't feel you should be spending money on yourself but genuinely from an affordability perspective, keep an eye out on the likes of Groupon for special deals or ask for vouchers for your birthday. Chapter 20 does tell you how to have a spa day at home, which includes some of the treatments you might go to a salon for but part of the reason this self-care tip is about going to a salon for a beauty treatment is that it is getting you to recognise the fact that spending money on yourself is not an extravagance but a necessity in order to recognise your self-worth. It is all relative though so if you have limited disposable income then opting for an at-home version is of course perfectly acceptable.

If you are someone who already visits the salon on a regular basis then fantastic, just make sure you are getting the treatments done because they make you feel good. If you feel that perhaps you are choosing treatments for another reason, try a new treatment just to make you feel good rather than look good. Perhaps go for a funky nail colour that you wouldn't usually opt for, for fear of what people might think. Or skip the spray tan for a relaxing massage instead.

The Short Version

- Beauty treatments are often people's go-to when they think of self-care but it is important to recognise and understand your reasons for visiting, or avoiding, a beauty salon.

- Taking care of your appearance is an act of self-love, not vanity, provided you are doing so for you and not for others.

- Although you can opt for at-home treatments, professional treatments will give you a better result and so are worth the expense, provided you can afford them.

Chapter 7
Get dressed up

"Give a girl the right kind of shoes, and she will rule the world." Marilyn Monroe

The Why

I'm writing this at a time when most of the world has spent the last year in some form of lockdown and a lot of us have spent that time working from home. This means that there has been limited requirements for making an effort to get dressed up beyond putting on a semi-smart top for the endless Teams meetings and Zoom calls. As lockdown has eased though, I have found the opportunity to dig out some of my nicer clothes, surprised that they still fit (well, most of them), and give them an outing – even if most of the time they are hidden under layers of coats and blankets thanks to the *al fresco* nature of our social lives. And I had forgotten how good it feels to make an effort with my appearance, rather than living in jeans. I have also come to realise that what I wear affects my confidence at work. Putting on my smart Hobbs dress for a meeting or presentation was part of my pre-COVID work ritual that definitely helped me to feel more confident. So, I have also taken to making more of an effort for the more important virtual meetings I have to attend – not to the extent that I will put on one of my "meeting in London" dresses – more swapping my daily uniform of jeans and a jumper for a skirt and a smarter top. And it does make a difference. Research has shown that dressing more formally can make us feel more confident[5], improve our level of focus[6] and increase our levels of abstract thinking[7].

One explanation for why what we wear can impact our confidence and performance is that dressing in certain ways leads to certain preconceptions. For example, the research into the effect of clothing on our focus levels found that those participants who wore a white lab coat while undertaking certain cognitive tasks had more

---

5   "The Clothing Makes the Self", Hannover, B. and Kühnen, U., Journal of Applied Social Psychology (2002)

6   "Enclothed cognition", Hajo Adam, Adam D. Galinsky, Journal of Experimental Social Psychology, Volume 48, Issue 4, 2012, Pages 918-925

7   'The Cognitive Consequences of Formal Clothing', Slepian, M. L. et al. (2015), Social Psychological and Personality Science, 6(6), pp. 661–668

attention and focus but only if they were told the lab coat was a doctor's lab coat. If they were told it was a painter's coat or were not given an association at all, their focus levels did not increase. Therefore, dressing in the style that emulates the feeling or persona of how you want to feel or who you want to be is perhaps key. In the context of self-care, getting dressed up in clothes that you would usually only wear for the more important meetings and events will give you a confidence boost.

The How

As you may have guessed, it is possible to dress yourself happy. I remember when I was aged around 9 or 10, I had a pair of stripey dungarees that I absolutely loved and wearing them always made me happy. They were bright and cheerful and looking back they still make me smile. Sadly, as I got older my desire to fit in meant that my clothing got less bright and cheery and now the predominant colour in my wardrobe is navy blue. Recently though I bought a bright yellow jumper on a bit of a whim and although it is quite bright, I really love it and received lots of compliments when I wore it. It turns out that my stripey dungarees and bright yellow jumper are a form of what has become known as "dopamine dressing". Dopamine dressing is where you wear clothes that make you feel good and boost your confidence and wellbeing. These can be items of clothing that you have become to associate with positive outcomes and experiences. For example, the outfit you wore to a successful job interview or a jumper you wore on a memorable day out with friends. They may also be items of clothing that you just feel great in – your favourite pair of jeans that you always look good and feel comfortable in no matter the time of month or the top that clings in all the right places and none of the wrong ones. And colour is part of this too. Bringing out these pieces of clothing when you need a bit of a mental boost is an easy self-care win. And when we feel good in what we are wearing, we are likely to look good as well, which can make us feel more confident and may even lead to a few compliments too. Wearing bright colours can help boost your mood too so, when you are feeling a little down, try to resist the urge to pull on that black or navy jumper and try a brighter option, such as pink, yellow or a bright blue. Another part of this is not caring what other people think. I love dungarees (even the non-stripey sort) but for years avoided my urge to wear them other than when pregnant or decorating because I was worried people would laugh at me. But eventually I got over myself and bought a pair of cool blue denim dungarees which I absolutely loved and each time I wear them it gives me a little spark of joy at the fact that I am doing so, even if people may laugh at me (most people didn't bat an eyelid and the one or two who did take the mick really didn't bother me). A key part of dressing happy is to be true to ourselves and our own sense of personal style and not let what others think get in the way. Doing so will result in a huge confidence boost and make you feel great.

The other aspect of making an effort to get dressed up is that it demonstrates that you are taking care of your appearance and are worthy of doing so. Often the only time I make an effort with how I look is if I'm going out or have a Teams meeting that warrants straightening the back as well as the front of my hair! But every once in a while, I make the effort, even though I have no particular reason to do. Getting dressed up for yourself and nobody else is a great way to boost your self-worth while at the same time making you feel good about yourself. You don't even have to go all out – simply putting on some nice jewellery and some lip gloss or swapping the daily uniform of leggings and a t-shirt for a skirt and a pair of tights can be enough to give yourself a little boost.

So go raid the back of your wardrobe and find that little gem that you haven't worn for ages, do your hair, go bold with your make-up and feel like a new woman!

The Short Version

- What you wear makes a difference to how you feel.
- Dressing more formally can make you feel more confident and improve your focus.
- Try "dopamine dressing" by wearing clothes that make you feel good and boost your confidence and wellbeing.
- Opt for brighter colours to boost a low mood.
- Make an effort with your appearance – not for anyone else but just because.

Chapter 8
Drink water

"Water is the driving force of all nature."
Leonardo Da Vinci

The Why

I am sure you have read many times the importance of drinking more water. Pretty much every article that talks about healthy living extolls the virtues of hitting your eight glasses a day. But why is it so important? And why, when this is not a book about healthy living, is there a chapter devoted to it?

Well, it turns out that drinking plenty of water really does bring some health benefits. And anything that is as simple to do as drinking water (or at least as simple as that should be – more on that to follow!) and will make you feel healthier, has to be up there on the self-care hot list.

The benefits of drinking water

Water makes up around 60% of our body (although this can vary between 45-75%)[8] so it is a pretty important element of the human body. But what does it do? Well, it has quite a long task list, but notable items include regulating body temperature, aiding digestion, preventing constipation, carrying nutrients and oxygen to our cells, cushioning joints and stabilising our heartbeat[9]. Therefore, ensuring our bodies have enough water to get through its to do list is certainly important.

Let's be honest though, the above list seems a little abstract. So, what are the more tangible benefits of avoiding dehydration?

Various studies[10] have shown that even being just slightly dehydrated can affect how your brain performs. This includes affecting your memory, as well as your mood[11], and impairing your brain's performance. It can make you less alert and cause you to feel fatigued.

---

8   "Dietary Reference Intakes for Water, Potassium, Sodium, Chloride, and Sulfate", Institute of Medicine, 2005, Washington, DC: The National Academic Press

9   "How much water should you drink?", Harvard Health Publishing, September 2016, updated March 2020

10   https://www.healthline.com/nutrition/7-health-benefits-of-water

11   "Influence of progressive fluid restriction on mood and physiological markers of dehydration in women.", Pross N, Demazières A, Girard N, et al., Br J Nutr., 2013;109(2):313-321

And it turns out that my go-to answer for whenever someone has a headache of drinking some water might well be good advice. There have been some studies that have shown that dehydration can cause headaches and that drinking additional water could help improve frequent headaches or migraines.[12] However, there is some debate over the link between headaches and water consumption so my advice may still need to be taken with a pinch of salt (although not literally!)

A well-known benefit of good levels of water consumption is that it helps relieve constipation. It can also help prevent it. And mineral water is even better as the magnesium and sodium in mineral water can help keep you regular.

And the list of reported benefits goes on, including helping to relieve kidney stones, increase sporting performance and helping with weight loss. And maybe I shouldn't admit this, but perhaps the one I rely on most frequently is that it can help prevent, and cure, a hangover! This is because alcohol is a diuretic and so causes you to lose more water than you consume. So, drinking that big glass of water before bed can help relieve the effects of dehydration, such as a headache and dry mouth in the morning.

---

12   https://www.healthline.com/nutrition/7-health-benefits-of-water

The How

How much water should I be drinking?

Well, I mentioned at the start of this chapter that you hear a lot about needing to drink eight glasses a day. Not only has this always flummoxed me slightly as I have no idea how big those eight glasses should be, but it's not actually true. There is no set quota you should be drinking each day. You just need to ensure you are drinking enough to not be thirsty. Your body is quite clever at telling you what it needs, so ensuring that you drink at the first sign of thirst or, even better, keep on top of your water intake to stay slightly ahead of your thirst, is all you need.

This self-care tip isn't about trying to hit a magic number when it comes to drinking water. It is to ensure you take the time to pause every now and again to check if you are thirsty. And then taking the time to have a drink. Don't say to yourself, I'll just finish writing this email and then go get some water. You'll finish that one and then another one will pop up and before you know it you've been sat there another hour with no drink and the beginnings of a headache.

And it doesn't have to be plain old water. Not that I am knocking plain water but, personally, unless it's cold I find it hard to motivate myself to drink water straight from the tap (and yes, I know I could put a jug of said tap water in the fridge but that's just one more thing I would have to remember to do). You can jazz up your water with a slice of lemon and/or cucumber. Or you can buy one of those fancy water bottles that you can put fruit in to flavour your water.

Tea and coffee also count but try to limit the amount of caffeine (see chapter 25) and opt for more herbal and fruit teas. I never used to be a fan of herbal teas – they all tasted too much like an actual hedgerow to me. But they have improved massively over the years and I quite enjoy them now (but still stay away from any that contain rosehip!) The Turmeric Active tea from Pukka Teas is one of my favourites and the Liquorice and Peppermint is great for when you want something sweet after dinner.

But why is it so hard to drink more water?

It sounds so easy, doesn't it? Drink more water. But it's really not – at least not for me. I have all these good intentions but get to the end of a workday and the pint glass of fizzy water I poured myself at the start of the day still sits there half drunk and flat. So how do you drink more water?

As with a lot of things, it comes down to making it a habit. Try and think of another activity you can link it to, which can act as a trigger. At first you will need to consciously remember to recognise the trigger but after a while (experts on habit creation have differing views on how long it takes for something to become a habit but between 21 and 30 days is a popular view), it will become a habit and you won't have to think about it and it will just happen naturally. For example, every time you click on your emails, have a drink before reading the latest arrival in your inbox. That only works if you are in the habit of checking emails frequently rather than batching your tasks (which is a much better way to manage your time and improve your productivity but that's another book).

If you are a regular tea or coffee drinker, have a glass of water while you wait for the kettle to boil. Leave a glass next to the kettle to remind yourself. This also works well first thing in the morning to encourage you to have some water when you first wake up. If you want to take it a step further, treat your tea or coffee as a reward – one that you only get if you have first had a glass of water. If you have to be on a lot of calls throughout the day, treat hanging up as a trigger to have a drink.

Experiment though and see what works for you. And don't forget about the weekends. This is probably my worst time for keeping hydrated because I don't have the triggers listed above and no set routine. And I confess,

I may well have had a drink (or two!) the night before so am even more likely to be dehydrated. So, think about triggers you can use at the weekend. Maybe it's each time you hear the kids shouting "Mummy!" (okay, that may be too much!) or each time you reach for your phone to scroll through Facebook or Instagram.

And if linking it to another activity doesn't work, set an alarm to remind you. You can also get various apps that encourage you to create healthy habits, including drinking enough water, and will give you a regular nudge to go get a glass of the good stuff.

The Short Version

- Drinking water is an easy way to look after yourself and reap the health benefits being fully hydrated brings.

- Water has a myriad of functions within the body, including regulating body temperature, aiding digestion, preventing constipation, and carrying nutrients and oxygen to our cells.

- There is no magic number of glasses you need to hit each day. Just drink enough to ensure you don't feel thirsty.

- Try adding lemon or other fruits to jazz up your water and opt for more herbal teas rather than lots of tea and coffee.

- Try and make drinking water a habit by linking it to another activity, such as checking emails, or don't let yourself check Facebook or Instagram without having had a glass of water.

Chapter 9

Have a rest day

"Almost everything will work again if you unplug it for a few minutes…including you."
Anne Lamott

The Why

People say that Sunday is the day of rest. But most working mums, or any mums at that rate, would say it certainly is not. It is just another day of running around after people, playing taxi, planning the week, doing the grocery shopping, washing and ironing school uniform, catching up on some work, cleaning out the pets your children promised they would look after… The list goes on! And that could be any day, not just a Sunday! In today's busy world we very rarely get a rest day, unless we are on holiday. But taking time out is so important.

I never quite appreciated how busy life was until the

first lockdown hit. Only when the running around and ferrying children about stopped, as well as all the socialising and travelling for work, did I realise that I was always on the go. And it felt good to have some downtime at the weekends. There was still plenty to do at the weekends, like preparing for the week's home schooling, catching up on work thanks to said home schooling and the usual washing mountain to conquer. But because we weren't going out anywhere, it felt like I had more time to fit it all in. And there was even the odd Sunday where I found the time to sit and read a book and it was great! But since coming out of lockdown things have got busy again so I've not had that downtime and I can definitely feel it.

They say a rest is as good as a holiday and I believe there is a lot of truth in that. Allowing yourself a day to completely relax really does help recharge the batteries and is something we should all be doing regularly. Taking time out, and I mean proper time out, can help reduce stress and, although it may seem counter-intuitive, increase productivity. It's easy to get stuck in the cycle of being constantly on the go but eventually all that busy-ness will catch up on you. Taking regular rest days prevents that from happening and you will feel so much better for it afterwards. How many times have you come back from holiday realising you didn't know how much you needed it? Try taking a proper rest day once a month and see if you have the same feeling.

The How

Now, if you are like me, you're probably sat there thinking that sounds great but it just ain't gonna happen. Who would feed the kids/dog/cat, do the washing, play taxi service, cook the dinner, tidy the house etc? Well, the answer is either someone else or no-one! Try and pick a day when there are no family commitments or, if there are, see if you can find someone else to do the rugby/football/tennis/ballet run. You could offer to take their child the following week to give them a break. And if your kids aren't old enough to feed themselves, ask your partner to feed them, if you have one, or treat yourselves to a meal out. The washing and ironing can wait or, if they can't, do it the day before. And work can definitely wait until an actual workday!

I'm sure though that some of you will still be sat there coming up with a million reasons as to why it's just not feasible. But are they reasons or excuses? Is the real reason you "*can't*" take a day out is that you would feel too guilty doing so? I find it incredibly hard, especially if I see my husband doing something around the house and I'm sat there reading my book. It's a common theme and one that can be quite challenging to overcome. As always though, it comes down to giving yourself permission to be "selfish" and to spend time on you. And understanding the reason as to why it is so important you do. A frantic, burnt-out you is no good to anyone – not your kids, not your partner, not your colleagues and certainly not you. If the thought of a whole day is too much then start with just an afternoon or morning.

Or maybe you're thinking you wouldn't know what to do with yourself. It can be hard to stop and relax when you are so used to being on the go. You basically just need to do something that you find relaxing and that will allow you to escape the day-to-day for a few hours. So perhaps read a trashy romance or gripping thriller. Watch your favourite movie with your favourite snacks or binge-watch your guilty pleasure on Netflix. Or go explore somewhere you've not been before or visit a museum or art gallery. You could even go to a spa or get your nails done and then have lunch in a nice café. And if you're really stuck, just think what you would do if you were on holiday (but perhaps not sunbathing in your bikini if the only place you can do this is the local park in the middle of winter!)

The key thing is that you take some regular time out for you. Put a recurring appointment in your calendar and stick to it – you really will feel rejuvenated when you keep that date with yourself.

The Short Version

- A rest is as good as a holiday so make sure you have a regular rest day or half day.
- Put it in your calendar and don't let it get bumped.
- Spend the time doing something you enjoy, whether that's reading a book, watching a film or going out for lunch.
- Do not under any circumstances do any housework, work or other tasks on your to do list.

Chapter 10
Improve your sleep habits

"Two hours of sleep before midnight is better than one after." Parents everywhere

---

The Why

I have always been someone who needs a good eight hours' sleep a night. And if I don't get a good night's sleep then everyone around me knows it! I vividly remember hitting a brick wall when my eldest daughter was a couple of months old when I just couldn't function due to the lack of sleep. Luckily my husband was able to take some time off work to let me try and get some sleep in the bank. And it's not the long hours at work during busy times that gets to me, it's the lack of sleep that accompanies that – whether that's due to burning the candle at both ends or waking up in the night worrying about it. And it is usually quite easy to recognise the impact sleep deprivation has on you – the overwhelming feeling of tiredness, the inability to concentrate, slower thinking and general moodiness – and to pinpoint a lack of sleep as the culprit. However, what is less obvious to spot is when you are getting enough hours but the quality of your sleep isn't so good. This is where healthy sleep habits come in – it's not always about how much sleep you get but how good a sleep it is.

There are so many reasons why getting a proper night's sleep is important for your self-care. Poor sleep habits can lead to disruption in our circadian rhythms, which has been shown to have all sorts of side-effects, both physical and mental. As well as fatigue, other effects of a short-term disruption of our circadian rhythms include a loss of concentration, impaired wellness and less energy and willpower to do some exercise or make healthy food choices. More long-term disruption has been associated with premature mortality, obesity, impaired glucose intolerance, diabetes, psychiatric disorders, anxiety, depression and cancer progression.[13] Various other studies point to a link to diabetes and infertility.

It is the deep sleep that provides our body with a chance to fully restore itself and to build up its defences against

13   https://www.karger.com/Article/FullText/500071

disease. Perhaps the scary thing is that some studies have shown that some people develop a tolerance for chronic sleep deprivation and so are not even aware of the effects a lack of sleep is having on them because it has become their norm.

The How

Reading about all the side-effects above is probably enough to stop anyone sleeping at night! So how exactly do you improve your sleep habits?

The first thing people tend to consider is whether they are getting enough sleep. But how long is enough? This varies from person to person but is usually between seven and nine hours per night. To find out what your optimum level is, try experimenting with different timings to see what works best for you. Do you wake up feeling refreshed and ready to start the day after just seven hours? Or, on the flipside, if you spend nine hours in bed do you feel sluggish and unable to get going? If so, you may be getting too much sleep (yes, there is such a thing!)

However, you do need to take into account the quality of your sleep when working out how much you need. Seven hours of good quality sleep is probably going to serve you better than nine hours of poor-quality sleep. So before declaring yourself as needing the full nine hours, carry out a sleep habit audit to see how good a quality sleep you are getting.

How many of the following questions can you answer "Yes" to?

1. I go to bed and get up at the same time each day, even at weekends or on holiday.
2. I eat healthily.
3. I exercise daily.
4. I spend at least 30 minutes outside each morning.
5. I don't nap after 3pm.
6. I don't drink caffeine after 12pm.
7. I don't drink alcohol after 7.30pm.
8. I eat my dinner at least three hours before bed.
9. I reduce my fluid intake in the evening.
10. I do not exercise within 2-3 hours before bedtime.
11. I dim the lights in the evening as part of my bedtime routine.
12. I have a hot bath an hour before bedtime.
13. I have a bedtime wind-down routine which sees me switching off at least 30 minutes before bedtime.
14. I stop using screens at least 30 minutes before bedtime.

15. I avoid stressful conversations close to bedtime.
16. My bedroom is a quiet, calm and relaxing space.
17. My bedroom is in complete darkness when I am sleeping.
18. My mattress and bedding are good quality and under eight years old.
19. My bedroom is cool, around 16-18°C.
20. If I don't fall asleep within 20 minutes, I do something calming like reading or listening to music. I don't look at my phone.

If you said "Yes" to 15 or more then that is pretty good going. Any less than that then you may want to make some changes.

For me, the biggest impact on the quality of my sleep is alcohol. I have a sleep app on my phone that measures the quality of my sleep via my smart watch and if I have had a few drinks in the evening, it significantly reduces the amount of deep sleep I get. Another factor that impacts my sleep is when I am stressed or worried about something. Those 4am wakeups where I can't get back to sleep. If you are finding that happening to you, do not reach for your phone (keep your phone in a different room at night to help with this). Instead, either try reading something or listening to some soothing music or, if that doesn't work, have a notepad and pen by your bed and write down what you are worrying about and why it is weighing on your mind. Once it is on paper you may find it easier to fall back to sleep.

If you have a smart watch or fitness tracker that has a sleep app, give it a try. It can be quite an eye-opener - being able to see the effect certain activities and environmental factors has on the quality of my sleep has certainly helped improve some of my sleep habits.

And if you still have trouble sleeping despite improving your sleep habits, do go see a doctor. Good quality sleep is such a vital part of taking care of yourself and is the gateway to so many other good self-care practices.

The Short Version

- A lack of sleep, particularly good quality sleep, can have a detrimental effect on both your physical and mental wellbeing.
- Not only is getting enough sleep important but so is ensuring it is good quality sleep.
- Develop good sleep habits by carrying out an audit of your bedtime routine and environment and making any necessary changes.

Chapter 11
Go out for breakfast

"I like breakfast-time better than any other moment in the day. No dust has settled on one's mind then, and it presents a clear mirror to the rays of things." George Eliot

---

The Why

One of the things I love about going on holiday is having breakfast out. We have been to Florida a few times and a regular trip to Denny's for pancakes is an absolute must. However, it's not something I think to do very often when at home, unless I'm away from home or it's a special occasion, like a birthday. Breakfast is not a family affair in our house – it's very much everyone grabs something as and when they need to. I tend to have it later in the morning, often while sat working at my desk, which I know is not ideal. Very rarely do I take the time to sit and enjoy a leisurely breakfast. The other day though I treated myself to breakfast at the local café and it felt so good to do something a bit different and to have someone else make breakfast for me. I went on my own and sat with my notebook doing some plotting and planning. I must iterate that I sat down in the café and ate my breakfast – I didn't do a take-away and take it back to my desk to eat. That's not the same. The key element is taking some time out to enjoy a nice breakfast, whether that is on your own, with your family or with a group of friends. Taking the time to stop and enjoy something that is part of your everyday life is an excellent form of self-care. We do so many of our daily activities on autopilot and get stuck in a routine that we often overlook how we might turn part of our daily routine, such as having breakfast, into a more enjoyable experience. Routines are important and having a daily routine can help prevent decision fatigue (see chapter 24). However, there are benefits to shaking up your routine[14], for example, by going out for breakfast. These benefits include the following.

More creativity

Taking a break from the norm gives your brain's neuroplasticity some exercise. But what is neuroplasticity? In essence, it is the way your brain connects the dots between your thoughts and the more "plastic" our brains

---

14   https://medium.com/work-life-success/https-medium-com-wrike-the-4-benefits-of-shaking-up-your-routines-fcdd5b27fa28

become, the more connections it is able to make. This in turn helps increase your creativity and problem-solving abilities. If you are having a mental block on something then heading to the local café for breakfast instead of grabbing your usual bowl of cereal may be just the thing that lifts that mental block.

Improved memory
A change in routine, in particular a change in location, stimulates our hippocampus, the area in the brain where long-term memories are stored. This can increase the brain's effectiveness and so, in turn, allow us to retain more information.

Better focus
Our brains are easily distracted and the modern world enables us to distract ourselves all too easily! The reason for this is that our brains are always seeking novelty so by mixing up our routine a little we give our brains the novelty they crave which in turn allows us to better focus on the task at hand.

Time to think
Not only does taking the time out to go out and have breakfast give us an opportunity to think, it also acts as a pause button on our daily routine, giving us space to re-evaluate that routine. Take the opportunity that sitting alone in a café with your breakfast gives you to think

about what is going well for you and which areas of your life you would like to change. This of course requires you to avoid multi-tasking while having your breakfast and to put your phone down but give it a go and see how it feels to have that time out in the day to just think.

The How

Like many of the tips in this book, the "how" is pretty self-explanatory – you simply go out for breakfast! But also like so many of these tips, the hard part is making the effort or finding the time to do it. This goes to the heart of self-care, namely that if we were talking about a breakfast meeting or a school breakfast fundraiser, you wouldn't hesitate to make the effort to go or juggle your other commitments to find the time to fit it into your busy schedule. But what message are you sending to yourself? That work or the school fundraiser is worth your effort and time but you are not. And to those of you who's response to that is that work and school are more important than swanning off for breakfast on your own, or that you would feel selfish for taking some time for you, or you would feel guilty as there are a million other things you "should" be doing, just stop. Stop seeing yourself as bottom of the pile when it comes to calls on your time and energy. Stop treating yourself as unimportant. Stop seeing time spent looking after yourself as being a waste of time. Instead, think about all the benefits spending some time with you brings. The boost to your mood that means you are less likely to snap at your children. The change in your life you could bring about by giving yourself the chance to stop and think. The increased creativity that a change of scenery or routine can bring. And just give it a go and see how you feel afterwards. And whether the world falls apart because you spent some quality time with a decent cup of coffee and a freshly baked croissant!

So, make the decision today to have a regular breakfast date with yourself. Put a date in your calendar so you block out the time and it is something to look forward to. When adding it to your calendar, write in where you are going to go for breakfast – this prevents you using not knowing where to go on the day as an excuse to stay at home with your bowl of cornflakes.

Try and leave your phone in your bag while enjoying your breakfast. Instead, try writing in a journal, reading a book or simply allowing yourself the time to daydream. And take your time – make the most of having some time to yourself. Don't treat it as just another item on the to do list to get ticked off as quickly as possible. You are on a date with yourself and bailing early on a date does not bode well in a relationship!

The Short Version

- Mixing up your routine by going out for breakfast is a great way to boost your mood, as well as your creativity, to improve your memory and focus, as well as giving you time to think.

- Make a date with yourself at your local café and treat that date with the same respect you would if it was a work breakfast meeting or school fundraiser.

- Accept that you are worthy of putting in the effort and finding the time to go out for breakfast.

- Make the most of the time by yourself when out for your breakfast by putting your phone away and reading, journaling or simply sitting there and thinking.

Chapter 12
Sign up for a subscription box

"Self–care is never a selfish act; it is simply good stewardship of the only gift I have, the gift I was put on earth to offer to others." Parker Palmer

The Why

Subscription boxes have become hugely popular over recent years and the range of boxes you can subscribe to is vast. From beauty products and clothes to coffee and stationery, there's a huge selection to choose from. You may well have given someone a gift of a subscription box. So why not give yourself a gift of one too? A few years ago, I signed up for Birchbox, which is a beauty subscription box and got very excited each month when the box arrived in the post. I have also been a subscriber of a clothing subscription service, Lookiero, where you get sent a selection of clothes each month and you can decide whether you want to keep them or not. The thing

I loved about these boxes, in particular the clothing one, is that they often contained items I would not have dreamt about buying for myself. A new shade of lipstick that would have terrified me in the shop but actually looked good once I tried it on. A dress that there is no way I would have chosen for myself but once I tried it on, I really loved. So not only did I give myself a regular treat, I was also expanding my horizons and getting to try new things (see chapter 35 for the benefits of trying something new). The other great thing was that I would often forget that they were due to arrive and so it would be a lovely surprise when they did and really brighten up my day.

You may be reading this and thinking how extravagant I am, subscribing to such things for myself. And to begin with I did feel the need to justify it. I only signed up to Birchbox initially because I got the first box free and then some more half price. I then only continued it because I thought the contents were handy for travelling and a good way to try different products before spending money on a full-size version (using the discount I got as a subscriber!) With Lookerio, I didn't actually have to keep any of the clothes but then I may as well keep at least one item because I would then get my £10 subscription fee back. And it saves me going to the shops. With the Papergang subscription I temporarily signed up to because a friend had a discount code, the contents were super useful (who doesn't need a drawer full of notebooks!) All these reasons are good reasons but, actually, the number one reason I should be keeping up with my subscription box is because I deserve it. Once again, it comes down to self-worth. Am I not worthy of a monthly treat? Are you not worthy? Would I think my best friend is worthy of a monthly gift? Then why not me? Or you? It doesn't have to be expensive, there are plenty of options out there that cost the same as a nice bottle of wine but it is a little nod to the fact that you recognise your own self-worth and are comfortable thinking of yourself as worthy.

The How

As I said above, there are lots of options for subscription boxes out there nowadays so it is really just a case of choosing one. Have a think about the sort of thing you buy yourself as a treat – is your go-to "pick-me-up" shopping item of choice a new lipstick, some new clothes, a foodie treat or anything in Paperchase? Use that as a guide to the type of box you would love to receive each month. Or is there a new hobby you want to try (or an old one you want to resurrect)? There are lots of hobby-based boxes too, such a crafty make or tasty bake.

I'd recommend going for a monthly delivery if you can, as that's frequent enough to not feel like an eternity until your next one, but not so frequent that you know when to expect it.

You can even use a subscription box to facilitate some of the other self-care tips in this book, such as home spa day (chapter 20), trying something new (see chapter 35) or read a book (chapter 40).

The Short Version

- A subscription box makes a great gift for a friend so why not treat yourself to one too – because you are most definitely worth it.

- Choose one that reflects what you would buy yourself as a treat or opt for one that encourages a new hobby or revives an old one.

- You can even combine a subscription box with another self-care practice in this book, such a reading a book or having a home spa day.

Chapter 13
Treat jar

"Nobody can be uncheered with a balloon." A.A. Milne

The Why

Sometimes it can be hard to decide which self-care activity you should do or even having to think of something to do is too much effort. Or perhaps you are feeling in a bit of a funk, a bit deflated and unmotivated and basically just can't be arsed to do anything, even something nice for yourself. Alternatively, you may just feel super stressed, frustrated or angry and just need a quick fix to jolt you out of it. For times like these, it's useful to have a treat jar on stand-by. A treat jar is, quite literally, a jar filled with "treats". These treats are self-care activities written on a piece of paper and folded up, ready for you to pick one out when the need arises. All you then have to do is pull out a piece of paper and do what it says. So, although some effort is required upfront, minimal effort is required to come up with a self-care activity in your time of need.

We've all had days where we are just not in the mood to do anything. Often, we know we need to do something to shift ourselves into gear but when you are in that mood everything feels like too much effort or uninspired. You might be able to come up with a whole list of things you could do but making a decision as to which one to do is just too much. Having a treat jar takes all the effort out of it. And requires very little motivation. All the thinking has been done ahead of time to come up with the activities. And there is no decision that has to be made, a critical aspect of the treat jar, because you simply do the first thing you pick out of the jar.

The How

Simply grab some paper, a pen, some scissors and a jam jar (or other suitable receptible) and start writing out your treats and putting them into your jar.

The treats in the treat jar should be ones that don't take too much effort to set-up or implement because, if you are using the jar as a go-to for when you can't really be bothered, then you are unlikely to be inclined to put much effort into the actual activity. They should also be quick pick-me-ups, effectively a bit of a kick-starter activity, which will be enough to make you feel better and perhaps even enough to kick-start another bigger self-care activity.

You can be as creative as you want with the treats that go into your jar but below is a list of some ideas to get you started:

1. Go for a 20-minute walk
2. Meditate for 10 minutes
3. Have a 20-minute power nap
4. Read a chapter of a fiction book
5. Give your child/other half/dog/cat/favourite chicken a cuddle
6. Go sit outside for 10 minutes
7. Read a magazine
8. Watch an episode of your favourite TV show
9. Go buy yourself a nice coffee/tea
10. Go buy yourself some flowers
11. Make up a jug of water with fruit in and drink it somewhere quiet
12. Light a candle
13. Put on your favourite song and sing at the top of your voice
14. Put on your favourite song and dance like nobody is watching
15. Phone a friend

16. Plan a night out with your partner
17. Bake something
18. Knit five rows of your current knitting project
19. Complete 10 pieces of your jigsaw
20. Do 10 star jumps
21. Paint your nails
22. Do a face mask
23. Do 10 minutes of yoga
24. Write in your journal
25. Do a random act of kindness (see chapter 38 for some ideas)
26. Tidy your workspace/bedroom
27. Change into your favourite outfit
28. Go buy something nice for lunch/dinner
29. Eat some fruit
30. Have a bath

The above are just some ideas to get you started, so make sure you tailor your treats to be things you would actually enjoy doing and try to come up with as many as possible. It's best to do this when you are in a positive frame of mind so one to prepare ahead for. You can also add to your jar as you come across new activities that make you feel good or new self-care ideas you read about.

When it comes to picking out an activity, you need to set some ground rules. Write them down and stick them to the underneath of the jar lid. The main rule (and probably the only one!) is how many "goes" you are allowed. If you're in a downbeat mood then the temptation will be to declare each treat you pull out as not something you want to do and you'll keep doing that until they have all gone! Depending on the nature of your treats, you could be quite draconian and state that you have to do the first one you pick out of the jar. However, if there are some treats in there that may not always be suitable, such as going outside when it is chucking it down with rain, you could allow yourself the "best of three".

Finally, don't feel you need to wait until you are feeling in a funk to use your treat jar – use it any time you want to. The more often the better!

The Short Version

- Sometimes you lack the motivation or inclination to practice some self-care, even though you know it would help lift you out of your slump.

- Having a treat jar means you can easily come up with a self-care treat without any effort or decision-making required.

- To make a treat jar, simply fill a jar with different self-care activities written on bits of paper.

- Choose activities that are easy to do.

- Add a note to the lid of the jam jar stating how many "goes" you get – do you have to do the first one you choose or do you, for example, get to choose the best of three?

Chapter 14
Make your bed

"If you want to change the world, start off by making your bed." William H. McRaven

---

The Why

I confess to historically being someone who never made their bed properly when they got out of it – it wasn't something that was drilled into me when I was young so it never became a habit. Then I read a couple of things that changed that. The first was a book called "Make Your Bed", by William H. McRaven, an ex-US Navy SEAL. In this book, which is based on the Commencement speech he gave to the graduating class of the University of Texas, he says, *"If you make your bed every morning, you will have accomplished the first task of the day. It will give you a small sense of pride and it will encourage you to do another task and another and another.*

By the end of the day, that one task completed will have turned into many tasks completed. Making your bed will also reinforce the fact that little things in life matter. If you can't do the little things right, you will never do the big things right. And, if by chance you have a miserable day, you will come home to a bed that is made—that you made—and a made bed gives you encouragement that tomorrow will be better. If you want to change the world, start off by making your bed."

The second thing I read was a post by Mel Robbins who talked about how she made her bed each morning as a gift to herself. What she meant by this, I believe, was that it was something she did for herself, rather than anyone else, which most of her other morning tasks had been for historically. It was also gift to herself for when she came to get into bed in the evening, she got to climb into a beautifully made bed. Lastly, along the same lines as William H. McRaven's philosophy, it was a gift in that it means she starts the day by completing a task and that sets her in the right frame of mind to accomplish other tasks throughout the rest of the day.

Now Mel's bed looks way nicer than mine – it has gorgeous bed linen and loads of beautiful cushions. But I now make an effort each morning to make my bed properly and I have to say, in the evening it is so much nicer to get into a well-made bed. It is on my to-do list to get some cushions to add to my bed and to treat myself to some nicer bed linen but even just my plain old bedding and pillow combo feels much more inviting having been nicely made in the morning.

The How

In short, you simply need to make it a morning habit, if it isn't already, to spend just a few minutes taking some care over making your bed – you will feel better for it and will appreciate it when you get to climb back into it in the evening. And, when you feel in need of an extra pick-me-up, change your bedding, even if it isn't due a change, and enjoy the extra special feeling of climbing into freshly washed bedding. It's even better if you have treated yourself to a relaxing bath (see chapter 1) beforehand too!

In terms of how to actually make a bed, I'm sure you know how to do this but if you want a five-star hotel worthy made-up bed then there are plenty of YouTube videos out there for you to watch. My basic approach is less involved with fewer sheets and cushions but is more than just roughly realigning the duvet. I start by throwing back the duvet to give the bed some air. I then take a moment to check the sheet is still nicely tucked in (not always the case as I seem to move around a lot in my sleep!), both along the sides and on the corners.

Next, I plump the pillows and line them up straight. I also neatly fold my pyjamas and place them just below my pillow, so they are there ready and waiting for me in the evening, rather than in a crumpled mess on the floor. I then give the duvet a good shake and straighten it out, making sure there is an equal overhang on each side to avoid duvet-stealing accusations from my husband. Finally, I'll lay the throw that sits on top of the duvet neatly along the bottom of the bed. This whole process takes less than five minutes but it does feel good to do.

And, if you have children that are old enough, start encouraging them to make their beds in the morning too – it's a fantastic habit for them to get into and, who knows, it may be their first step on a journey to change the world.

The Short Version

- Both William H. McRaven, an ex-US Navy SEAL, and Mel Robbins, have written about the benefits making your bed each day can bring.

- These include the sense of accomplishment of completing your first task, as well as it being something you do for yourself, rather than anyone else.

- Try and take that extra five minutes each morning to properly make your bed and you will feel grateful you did when you slip back into it in the evening.

Chapter 15
Get outside

"Some old-fashioned things like fresh air and sunshine are hard to beat." Laura Ingalls Wilder

---

The Why

If you are anything like me during our recent periods of lockdown, enforced working from home and home-schooling, there were times when a whole day went by without you leaving the house. The school run was no longer a thing and, once the novelty of the government-mandated daily walk wore off, the extra busy days left me neglecting my lunchtime dog walk. So, the good thing about the end of home-schooling (beyond the obvious!) is that it means I do at least leave the house to do the school run. It may only be a five minute walk each way but it does at least force me to get some fresh air, no matter what the weather!

And getting outside in the fresh air is so important for self-care for many reasons. Firstly, it helps boost your Vitamin D levels, especially if you can expose more than just your face to the sun (not quite so easy in the winter months but more achievable in the summer months – well, some of the time!). Vitamin D is important for all sorts of things, including your blood cells, bones and immune system. Sunlight helps boost your serotonin levels, which in turn helps boost your mood and energy levels. And, if you're able to get outside in the morning, in particular, it can help regulate your sleep cycle, leading to improved sleep.

It can also be a good for when you are stuck on a problem you're trying to solve or struggling to come up with something creative. Studies have shown that time spent in nature can help improve your problem-solving capabilities. Even just stepping outside for a few minutes can be enough to reset your thinking.

The How

Make sure you spend some time outside each day, ideally for at least half an hour. If that feels like a lot of time to build into your day, try and combine it with another activity, such as exercise or meeting a friend. With the influx of outdoor eating options, it's easier now than ever to meet for a coffee or lunch outside and enjoy the benefits of the fresh air. If it's warm enough, take a few minutes out of your morning to sit outside with a coffee or some time in the afternoon to enjoy a cup of tea outside. An early morning walk is a great way to start your day as it gets your blood pumping, clears the cobwebs and gives you a dose of Vitamin D. In the summer evenings, a walk after dinner is a great way to enjoy the sunset and takes advantage of the cooler evening air. And you don't have to go for a walk (although walking is a good form of exercise), you can simply sit in your garden or local park and take in your surroundings or read your book – earning you self-care bonus points!

In the winter months, it can be more challenging to get outside. A lunchtime walk is a good option as it avoids the darker mornings or evenings. Although bracing, a walk on a cold, crisp morning, is fantastic to awaken the senses – and you will appreciate your cup of hot tea or coffee even more than usual when you return. Often, it can be harder to motivate yourself to get outside when it's cold, and even more so when it's wet and raining! So, at times like those, you might need to put in place a reward system for getting outside. For example, you might reward yourself with a posh hot chocolate (with cream and marshmallows!) if you walk to the local café to meet your friend, rather than drive.

Another great motivator is getting a step counter and setting yourself of hitting the recommended 10,000 steps a day. While you can pace around your living room (not that I have done that to hit my target, honest!), the steps will go up a lot quicker if you go for a walk round the block to tip yourself over the 10,000 mark.

The Short Version

- There are many health benefits to getting outside, from the Vitamin D boost to the improved sleep pattern.
- Find ways to build in time outside to your daily routine, whether it's an early morning walk, a lunchtime stroll or an *al fresco* dinner with friends.

Chapter 16
Leave your desk

"Life requires movement." Aristotle

The Why

If, like me, you spend most of your time sat at a desk then this one is for you. It wasn't until I got an Apple watch that tells me off if I've been sat down for an hour without moving that I realised just how little I got up from my desk during the day. And just how quickly an hour passes when you are engrossed in something. And it wasn't until I read about how important it is to keep moving throughout the day that I made more of a conscious effort to get up and walk around more regularly during the course of a workday.

There have been several studies[15] that have shown the risks associated with a sedentary lifestyle. In 2015, a large review of studies on the topic in the Annals of Internal Medicine found that even after adjusting for physical activity, sitting for long periods was associated with worse health outcomes including heart disease, Type 2 diabetes and cancer. It has also been shown to increase blood pressure and raise cholesterol[16]. Then of course there is the risk of weight gain and obesity. For women in particular, a sedentary lifestyle has been cited as one of the factors that can impact fertility[17] and those facing the menopause have been shown to experience more severe menopausal symptoms and depressive symptoms, anxiety and insomnia if they lead a sedentary lifestyle[18]. And the list goes on!

What surprised me most is that you can't counteract that with a blast at the gym or on the exercise bike at the end of the day. Although high levels of exercise can reduce the risks associated with a sedentary lifestyle, if you are

---

15 https://www.hopkinsmedicine.org/health/wellness-and-prevention/sitting-disease-how-a-sedentary-lifestyle-affects-heart-health

16 "Sedentary Lifestyle and Cardiovascular Health.", Kim SY, Korean J Fam Med. 2018;39(1):1

17 "Sedentary lifestyle and risk of obesity and type 2 diabetes.", Hu FB, Lipids. 2003 Feb;38(2):103-8

18 https://www.researchgate.net/publication/292154076_Sedentary_lifestyle_in_middle-aged_women_is_associated_with_severe_menopausal_symptoms_and_obesity

still sitting for 10 hours or more the rest of the day then your risk of cardiovascular disease increases. So, whilst ensuring you are getting regular exercise is important, it is equally important to ensure you are regularly taking steps – literally – to get up from your desk or from in front of the TV.

The How

But how do you ensure you are moving enough? There are several ways you can approach this. If you have a smart watch or step counter, a lot of these will have a way of setting alerts for when you have been sedentary for a period. If you don't have one of these, you can set an alarm to remind you to get up and have a walk around. If you're not keen on the idea of an alert or an alarm, you can try combining activities. For example, each time you make a phone call, stand up and walk around. Or, if you can't walk around while on a call (not quite so feasible now most calls seem to be video calls!) then make it a habit to get up and walk around after your call. Or, better still, do some star jumps (maybe one for the home office!)

Look at ways you can build movement into your everyday activities. If you are driving into work, try parking a bit further away – be that another car park (which may have the added bonus of being cheaper than your usual one) or even opting for a car park space the furthest from your office entrance. Take the stairs rather than the lift. Go see your colleague in the next building rather than calling or emailing them. Or walk the long way round to the toilet. If you work at home, it can often be harder to build in those extra movement activities but try walking round the block before and after work faux-commute style. Or, if you work downstairs and have a choice of a toilet upstairs or downstairs, go for the upstairs one.

And don't forget about keeping up the movement in the evenings. It can be very tempting, once you have finally sat down in front of the TV or to read your book, to not get up again until bedtime. So, instead of fast-forwarding through the ads, get up and walk around while they are on. Or make yourself get up between chapters or Netflix episodes and, if you can't bear the thought of pausing between Bridgeton episodes, keep watching but stand up and do some stretches.

You can also combine this self-care activity with others. For example, getting outside ticks lots of boxes, including this one, so even more reason for a lunchtime walk. Drinking more water (chapter 8) is another one – when getting up to go get a glass of water and hot drink take a few extra minutes to walk around the room.

It really is quite simple to incorporate more movement

into your day, once you have worked out a suitable trigger, and has great health benefits.

The Short Version

- Leading a sedentary lifestyle has been associated with an increased risk of a number of health issues, including disease, Type 2 diabetes, obesity, depression and even cancer.

- You cannot counteract a sedentary lifestyle with bursts of activity at the gym – regular movement throughout the day is required.

- Look for ways to increase your movement, such as setting up notifications on your fitness tracker or smart watch, linking it to another activity such as hanging up the phone or build in more opportunities in your regular routine, like parking further from the office.

Chapter 17
Gratitude

"Gratitude is not only the greatest of the virtues
but the parent of all others." Cicero

The Why

You may have noticed that the concept of gratitude has become increasingly popular in recent years. There are now gratitude journals, gratitude apps and Instagram is full of quotes about gratitude. So, what's it all about?

Well, actually, it isn't really anything new. For centuries, people have been practicing gratitude in one form or another. In many religions, prayers have long been a way to give thanks to that religion's God. Thanksgiving in the United States is, as the name suggests, all about giving thanks. Sending thank you letters for gifts is a long-standing tradition for many people. However, what is new, is the study of the health and wellbeing benefits that being grateful brings to people.

These studies have found that practicing gratitude provides a number of health benefits. These include reducing feelings of stress, boosting the immune system, lowering blood pressure and improving sleep. It also enhances our wellbeing by increasing feelings of positivity and can help improve our mental health.

There have also been studies[19] looking at the link between gratitude and healthy eating. It is already relatively well-established in social psychology circles that feelings of positivity can help us make healthier food choices. Anyone who has hit the vending machine at work after a stressful meeting would support that hypothesis. What is less established is the impact that gratitude specifically has on our eating habits. The results from these studies suggested that practising gratitude on a regular basis can also help us make healthier food choices.

It's not clear yet why gratitude leads to healthier food choices but one theory is that practising gratitude increases positive feelings and reduces negative ones. As mentioned above, it's when we are feeling more negative about life that we tend to turn to less healthy food for

_____

19 https://www.sciencedirect.com/science/article/abs/pii/S0022103117308569

comfort. Any Bridget Jones fans can attest to this. So it may be that it's just the increase in feelings of positivity that results from practising gratitude that leads to better food choices - we are in a much better position to make healthy food choices when we are not feeling stressed, are in good health and not tired. My worst time for raiding the fridge is a Friday afternoon after a long and stressful week at work!

The How

Practising gratitude is, at its heart, very simple. It's just acknowledging the things in your life that you are grateful for. It doesn't have to take too long to do – just a few minutes each day will reap positive results. And you don't need any special tools or equipment to do it! Fundamentally, all that is required is for you to take a moment each day to stop and think about all the things in life that you are grateful for. But if it's so easy, how come so few of us do it? I think it's because it's not something we think about doing unless prompted. Unless we proactively seek to express or acknowledge what we are grateful for, we don't take the time to do so. There are though several ways to introduce gratitude into your life and some suggestions are as follows.

1. Use an app

I use one aptly named "Gratitude" but there are lots of

other apps out there that do the same thing. The beauty of an app is that it easy to do, you can set it up to remind you to use it and we are so used to doing everything else on our phones so why not this too?

The app enables you to easily record what you are grateful for and many have prompts to help you come up with ideas of what that might be. Things like, what was the best thing about today or what are you looking forward to? This can help when you are struggling to think of what you are grateful for, especially if, like me, you try to come up with new things each day.

2. Use a notebook

If you prefer getting out a pen and paper then find yourself a nice notebook to write down the things you are grateful for. There is something therapeutic about writing and, if, like me, you are a notebook-addict, it's a great excuse for another one! Or a good way to use one already in your collection. It's also lovely to be able to read back through it.

Have a think about how you will use your notebook. Did you want to use it to list out three or maybe five things that have been good that day? Or use it to write letters of gratitude to people who have had a positive impact on your life? Or even letters to yourself? There is no set way, so just go for whatever works for you.

And make sure you keep it somewhere you see it so you remember to use it.

3. Use a dedicated gratitude journal

Similar to the above, there are actually dedicated gratitude journals you can buy. The benefit of having a dedicated journal is that they include prompts to help you express your gratitude. They will also often encourage you to go a little deeper than simply listing out your top three things you are grateful for that day, so a good option if you want to delve a little deeper into the world of gratitude.

4. Gratitude jar

This is a great way to introduce children to the concept of gratitude. Although you can buy "proper" gratitude jars, you really just need a clean, empty jam jar. You then write on pieces of paper what you are grateful for and pop them into the jar.

Then, when you need a bit of a mood boost, pick one out of the jar and give it a read.

5. Set a reminder on your phone

One of the hardest things to do is to actually remember to think about what you are grateful for. So set a reminder on your phone to prompt you at the same time each day.

6. Share around the dinner table

Another one that is lovely to do with the children. Boost your dinner table conversation by asking everyone to say what they are grateful for. If that is a bit too abstract, especially for younger children, try using different prompts. For example, what was the best thing that happened that day. Or what made them laugh.

And you don't have to go for every mealtime if that's too much to aim for, particularly to start with. You could make it a Sunday lunch thing or Friday night dinner thing at the end of the week.

7. Do while brushing your teeth

Linking your gratitude practice to an already established habit will help you to also turn gratitude into a habit. Use brushing your teeth as a trigger to think about what you are grateful for. Or grab your journal or open your gratitude app when you sit down with your first cup of tea or coffee of the day.

Or make it part of your kids' bedtime routine – a lovely way to send them off to the land of nod.

8. Start small

Like anything new, practising gratitude can take, well, practice! It takes time to turn something into a habit. It also takes time to change your mindset into one that is always looking for the positive. When you have had a tough day, it can be challenging to come up with one, let alone three things to be grateful for.

So don't beat yourself up if you can only think of one thing a day to start with. Or if you don't manage to practise every day. Start off small and build it up and after not too long it will become second nature.

9. Challenge yourself to be original

It's easy to trot off the usual list of things we are grateful for. Our children, our other half, our family, our health, our home… And of course, if they are all good in our life, they are things we should definitely be grateful for.

Being more specific though deepens the sense of gratitude. It makes it more personal and relevant to us as individuals. So instead of being grateful for your home, try and think of specific details. Do you love the way the light falls in the kitchen in the morning? Does the stack of cushions you have on your bed bring you joy?

And try not to repeat the same things each day. It is easy to fall into the trap of picking the easy ones. Like hugs from my children – I love these and they do make my day and I am extremely grateful for them. But not letting myself use that as one of my things to be grateful for every night forces me to think of other things. Like seeing my son's face as we reach an exciting part in a story we are reading together. Or my daughter sharing the detail of her day with me – rather than getting the usual three-word answer, "it was good".

10. Send a gratitude letter

Another powerful way to express gratitude is to write and send a letter of gratitude to someone. This has the added benefit of being a beautiful act of kindness and the perfect way to show someone you appreciate them. And if a letter feels too much of a challenge, a simple "thank you for being there" note or card is enough. It is sure to brighten the lucky recipient's day and give you a huge boost of positivity.

Some of the above suggestions may seem too much to you, especially if you are just getting started. Like anything though, once you make being proactively grateful a habit, it will become second nature to you and will no longer feel like an effort. And you may find you don't need to have an app or a special journal to practise gratitude once it has become a habit to do so. And do try and make it a habit. If not, the times when you need it most, like when you are feeling stressed or unhappy, you won't have the motivation to force yourself to see the positives. If you have made it into a habit, you are more likely to continue your practise during more challenging times. And if you are struggling to find anything to be grateful for, just remember there is always an "at least" in life (see chapter 21).

The Short Version

- Gratitude has been around for centuries but has become more popular in recent years due to its reported health and wellbeing benefits. These include reducing feelings of stress, boosting the immune system, lowering blood pressure and improving sleep.
- Introducing a daily practise of gratitude can bring about some of these health and wellbeing benefits.
- Simply spend some time each day thinking about what you are grateful for.
- You can try using a dedicated gratitude app, a notebook and pen or writing a letter to someone (or to yourself).
- If you have children, introduce them to the concept of gratitude by asking them what was good about their day at the dinner table or at bedtime.

Chapter 18
Sing your heart out

"He who sings scares away his woes." Miguel de Cervantes

The Why

I am a terrible singer. If I were to go on the X-Factor I would definitely make it through to the TV auditions for pure comedy value. Even my children tell me to stop singing if ever I sing along to the radio! But when I need to let off some steam, I find turning up the volume of the music in my car and singing at the top of my lungs works wonders.

And it's great for all sorts of scenarios. If I'm angry about something then something shouty like Alanis Morrisette's, "You Oughta Know" is fantastic for letting off some steam, as is Meredith Brooks', "Bitch". If I need a boost of confidence on the way to work then Rachel Platten's, "Fight Song" is my go-to song. And there's plenty of options for when I just need a little pick-me-up, from Black-Eyed Peas, "I Gotta Feeling" to Ed Sheeran's, "Galway Girl" – I feel so much better after belting out some of those.

As it turns out, there is some science behind why I feel so much better after some Car-a-oke. According to one study[20], people's cortisol levels are lower after singing, which shows they feel more relaxed after bursting into song. And apparently it doesn't matter if you are singing alone or in a group, which is good news for someone tone deaf like me! What does matter though is whether or not you are singing in a stressful environment. If you are having to perform to an audience then this can, as you might expect, increase your stress. So, another good reason for me to stick to my car as a venue.

There are also other reported health benefits, including boosting your immune system, improving lung function, increasing your pain threshold and even helping to reduce snoring! So, even more reason to make singing a daily part of life.

---

20   https://www.frontiersin.org/articles/10.3389/fpsyg.2015.01242/full

The How

If you're finding yourself feeling stressed, a bit low or in the need of a confidence boost, find somewhere you won't be heard (unless you have the voice of angel, in which you may not care about being heard), put on some familiar tunes and just sing-along.

I have a Spotify playlist I set up with all my favourite songs to put on when I need a bit of a boost or some motivation, which is something I would recommend. It just makes it easy to find that "one" song that will really put you in the right frame of mind, rather than spending the whole car journey flicking through the radio channels trying to find a suitable song. You can set up different playlists depending on the mood you are in – so one with uplifting music to boost your mood, another with power ballads to boost your confidence and one with rock music when you need to let off some serious steam!

The car is a great place to belt out some tunes, especially if you are driving solo. Then of course there is the old favourite of singing in the shower (not one I have been able to get on board with as it seems amplify my lack of tunefulness!) Sticking on some loud music and singing along while you clean the house is another great option – it somehow makes doing the cleaning slightly less painful (only slightly mind you – I am not a fan of doing the housework!)

If you have slightly more vocal talent than I do (or even if you don't but are willing to learn!), consider joining a local choir or singing group. And if there isn't one, why not set one up? Or grab some friends for a fun night out at the local karaoke bar or a night in with Let's Sing on the PlayStation – definitely no singing talent required for these last two suggestions!

The Short Version

- Singing along to your favourite songs is a great way to boost your mood, relieve some stress or crank up your confidence.

- There is scientific evidence that suggests singing can lower your cortisol levels, boost your immune system, improve lung function, increase your pain threshold and help reduce snoring.

- Set up a playlist that you can turn to when you feel the need to belt out a tune.

- Either go for the solo option in the car or in the shower or go more social with a karaoke night out or singalong PlayStation game at home.

Chapter 19
Tidy your desk

"Outer order contributes to inner calm."
Gretchen Ruben

The Why

If you are one of those super-organised and tidy people then you can probably skip this one. But if you are like me and the words "clear desk policy" strike fear into your heart, then read on!

I have never been particularly tidy, even as a child (although I'm not sure how many children are actually tidy!) But I do remember the sense of satisfaction I would get when I did finally decide to tidy my room (note the "when I decided" – not after being told to do so by my exasperated parents!) It would take me ages to do but I would do a great job and love the result –

everything in its right place and looking so decluttered. Fast-forward to my adult life and I confess to still living much the same way. I tend to take the "blitz" approach to housework – not being one to "keep on top of it", despite knowing that if I did it wouldn't then eat into my entire Saturday! Don't get me wrong, I do the necessary level of cleaning but "stuff" just seems to pile up and accumulate around the house. Every now and then though I hit breaking point and go all out with the tidying up (either that or we have guests coming!) And, once again, I feel so much better for it.

Whether you are a naturally tidy person does come down to your personality and, most probably, the environment you grew up in. And there is nothing wrong with being messy – some of the world's greatest minds reportedly fall in the messy desk camp, including Einstein, J K Rowling and Steve Jobs. A messy environment can even encourage creativity. But if you ever start to feel overwhelmed, try taking a look around you and see if perhaps your environment could be contributing to that feeling.

There have been various studies carried out that have shown a number of health and wellbeing benefits of decluttering your environment. One study[21] found that

---

21   "No Place Like Home: Home Tours Correlate With Daily Patterns

women who described their homes as "cluttered" were more depressed and fatigued. They also had higher levels of cortisol, that well-known stress hormone. Working in a tidy space can also help you make healthier food choices[22], with those working in a tidy office space twice as likely to reach for an apple than a chocolate bar. Another study[23] found that decluttering your workspace can boost your productivity, by reducing the number of things your visual cortex is forced to take in.

So even if you have a natural affinity to clutter, try out a less cluttered approach and see if you notice a change for the positive.

The How

As mentioned above, I have always had a tendency for the blitz approach when it comes to tidying up. And, as much as I would love to sit here and write about how I have now realised that the "keeping on top of it" approach is the right one, I would be lying. I am better when we've been lucky enough to have a cleaner coming

of Mood and Cortisol", Darby E. Saxbe and Rena Repetti, Pers Soc Psychol Bull 2010 36:71

22 "Physical Order Produces Healthy Choices, Generosity, and Conventionality, Whereas Disorder Produces Creativity", Kathleen D. Vohs, Joseph P. Redden, Ryan Rahinel, Psychological Science

23 "Interactions of top-down and bottom-up mechanisms in human visual cortex.", McMains S, Kastner S., J Neurosci. 2011 Jan 12;31(2):587-97

in, because I tidy up before they come (yes mum, I do, but I'm paying them to clean, not tidy!) but it is still always left to the morning they are due to come. But what I have pledged to do, since having my own little office space at home, is to keep my desk tidy. It's where I spend most of my week and I do notice a correlation between how stressed I am feeling and how messy my desk is. When I get really busy with work, I tend to have lots of bits of paper all over my desk with various notes on and the amount of desk that is visible gradually reduces. However, if I stop and take just five minutes to do some tidying up, I feel so much better. It restores a sense of calm over my working space and means I know where to find my various notes when I need them on a call, rather than having to scramble for them frantically – something that is harder to do now that every call seems to require video!

If you are also not one for the "little and often" approach to tidying and have let things get a little (or a lot) out of hand, then the thought of tidying it up is probably too overwhelming to even contemplate, so you don't. If this is the case, break it down into much more manageable tasks. Take one pile of papers / stuffed drawer / filing tray at a time and just clear that. Be ruthless in your clearing – do you really need all your paper bank statements from age 12? (Yes, until we moved house a couple of years ago, I still had all mine!) Invest in a mini shredder and get shredding!

Another tip is to try and tidy your workspace at the end of each working week. For me, this is a Friday, so spending just ten minutes at the end of the day clearing away the accumulation of papers and other assorted miscellany that has crept into my office during the course of the week, acts as a useful signal that work is now done for the weekend. That, coupled with my habit of writing out my to do list for the next working day before finishing my current day (see chapter 21), means I feel much more like I can draw a line underneath my working week, ready to start afresh after the weekend.

I've focused on keeping your desk tidy but the same applies to wherever you spend a lot of time.

So, the moral is, if you are not a naturally tidy person and/or a very busy one, don't put the extra pressure on yourself to keep the whole house tidy 24/7. Pick just one place where you spend most of your time, or a lot of your time, and keep that tidy. And it may well be that it plants the seed for tidiness elsewhere in your life.

The Short Version

- Keeping your immediate environment tidy can help prevent fatigue and depression and reduce stress levels.

- If ever you start to feel overwhelmed, try taking five minutes out to clear your working space – and your head.

- If the amount of clutter surrounding you feels like a mountain to climb, just take one pile of papers or a single drawer at time.

Chapter 20
Home spa day

"Every now and then go away, have a little relaxation, for when you come back to work your judgment will be surer." Leonardo da Vinci

---

The Why

I'm not sure there are many people who don't enjoy a trip to the spa. And, if you are able to treat yourself with a trip to an actual spa then that is a fantastic form of self-care! The costs of a spa day though can be prohibitive to many and is often saved for special occasions. That doesn't mean that you have to miss out on the experience of a spa day, because you can easily recreate one at home. And although you can't replicate a full-on traditional spa day at home (unless you happen to have a swimming pool, sauna and resident beauty therapist at home!), there are lots of things you can do at home to replicate the feeling of being at a spa.

That feeling is a feeling of being pampered and having the opportunity (and dare I say permission) to relax for the day – two things that most definitely score high on the self-care barometer. You want to leave a spa feeling refreshed, glowing and beautiful. And you want to have a reason to sit around in your dressing gown and slippers all day without being judged (or maybe that's just me!)

Allowing yourself a day, or half a day, where you focus on taking care of yourself and relaxing, is a key benefit of an at home spa day. It signals to your subconscious mind that you are wholly worth being pampered and taken care of, that you deserve to be and that acts as a great boost to your sense of wellbeing. It also forces you to stop and slow down, to relax and take it easy. This allows your body, as well as your mind, to rest and restore itself. And of course, the various treatments you choose bring their own benefits.

The How

So how do you turn your home into a spa for the day? Well, there's lots of things you can do, especially if you use your imagination, but below are a few ideas as a starter for ten. Make sure you don your dressing gown and slippers, being sure to advise other members of the household what you are up to (and who cares what the Amazon delivery driver thinks!) And try to get everything prepped in advance so that you can simply move between activities and treatments. Finally, light some candles and, if you fancy it, put on some soft music to help you relax.

Here are some ideas for you, in no particular order.

Foot Spa

Add some warm water to a suitable vessel (I used the washing basket!) and, if you have them, add some Epsom salts and essential oils (see chapter 1 for the benefits of these) or some bubble bath. If you don't have either of those things, you could add some fresh or dried rosemary or fresh or ground ginger (great for circulation), chamomile teabags (great for inflammation), lemon juice or vinegar (great for exfoliation) or honey or coconut milk (great for moisturising). Then, sit back and relax for at least 15 minutes – you can choose to read a book, listen to some music, meditate or just sit back and enjoy the peace and quiet. A good tip is to have a flask of hot water with you so you can top up your foot spa if it starts to cool. Once you have had enough soaking, rinse your feet in some clean, warm water and then moisturise.

Manicure and Pedicure

Giving yourself a pedicure is the perfect follow-on treatment to a foot spa. And when I say manicure and pedicure, I don't mean just slap some nail varnish on!

I mean going the whole hog – filing them into a nice shape, softening and tidying your cuticles and applying both a base and a top coat. I say this because, if you are anything like me, nail painting is usually a very slapdash affair that I attempt way too late in the day before an evening out, resulting in me using my teeth to pack my handbag to avoid smudging my nails! If all that sounds like a bit too much effort, you could instead arrange for a mobile nail technician to visit or bribe a child of sufficient competence to do it for you!

DIY Facial

When I think of a facial at home, it extends so far as slapping on a face mask for five minutes while I let my conditioner soak in. A full-on facial though follows all the different steps a proper facialist would follow, as set out below.

Step 1. Cleanse. And I don't mean a quick onceover with a cleansing wipe. I mean taking the time to fully cleanse your skin using a good cleanser. Make sure you concentrate on getting into all the nooks and crannies (aka creases!) and then rinse well with warm water. If you want to take it a step further, use an oil-based cleanser first to remove all your make-up and then a water-based cleanser to clear away any remaining dirt.

Step 2. Exfoliate. This helps to remove dead skin cells

and unblock pores, paving the way for the products you use next to absorb into the skin more easily. You can use a shop-bought exfoliator, which is the simplest option. Alternatively, you can make your own using oats, coconut oil and yoghurt. Simply grind down two tablespoons of oats in a blender until they resemble a fine power and then mix in a tablespoon each of plain Greek yoghurt and coconut oil. Oats have antioxidant and anti-inflammatory properties, yoghurt contains lactic acid, which can help enhance exfoliation and coconut oil is a great moisturiser[24]. There are also plenty of other homemade recipe ideas online.

Step 3. Face massage. Spend 10 minutes giving yourself a face massage (see chapter 26 for further guidance on how to do this).

Step 4. Face mask. Select a face mask suitable for your skin type and sit back and relax. Again, you can opt for a shop bought one or make your own. A mashed banana mixed with a tablespoon of honey is a good option for combination or dry skin. Banana is a great all-rounder, bringing a good mix of vitamins, including vitamins A, B and E, as well as moisturising potassium. Honey has lots of great properties, particularly if you splash out on some Manuka honey, including being naturally

---

24   https://www.healthline.com/health/homemade-facial-scrub

anti-bacterial, high in antioxidants and moisturising. And half an avocado blended with quarter of a peeled cucumber is great for oily skin. Avocado helps regulate oil production and cucumber is hydrating but also contains vitamin C, which helps prevent breakouts.

You can choose to take the time to read your book or simply lay back and relax, in which case add some slices of cucumber to your eyes. Yes, this is a quite stereotypical look but that is because it does work and there is some scientific evidence to back this up. Cucumber has a high vitamin C and folic acid content, which can boost new cell growth and stimulate antioxidants that help fight off the environmental toxins that can make eyes appear puffy or tired[25]. For best results, leave on your eyes for at least 15 minutes, which is usually about the right amount of time for your face mask to works its magic too.

Step 5. Tone. After rinsing off your face mask, it's time to use your favourite toner (or the one that has been sat on the shelf for a while as you keep forgetting to use it – or is that just me?!) The job of toner is to close and clean the pores, now that the face mask has done its work. It also helps to brighten skin tone. There are homemade toner ideas out there, if you would prefer to make your own. These include combining a third of a cup of cooled

---

25   https://www.healthline.com/health/cucumbers-on-eye

green tea with a few drops of tea tree oil, or a cup of cooled chamomile tea with a teaspoon of honey and two tablespoons of apple cider vinegar[26].

Step 6. Moisturise. This is the final step where you get to lather on your favourite moisturiser and, if you have any, a serum too (before your moisturiser). You may also want to add your eye cream to complete the pampering. And then you can step out of your bedroom/bathroom/lounge with that post-facial glow!

Bath time

Although not quite the same as getting to soak in a luxury pool or sit in a hot tub, having a candlelit bath is a great alternative. I cover the benefits of a bath in chapter 1 and set out there some tips on what to put in it and how to make it that bit extra special so I won't go over those again here. But to enhance the experience further, try adding a body scrub. As with the facial you can of course buy a nice body scrub but you can also make your own. For a sugar scrub, mixing two parts brown sugar to one part coconut oil is a good combination. And one that is becoming increasingly popular is a coffee-based scrub, which you can make by mixing together half a cup of coffee grounds with two tablespoons of water and a

---

26   https://www.healthline.com/health/beauty-skin-care/diy-toner

tablespoon of warmed coconut oil[27]. There's even some (albeit not 100% qualified) evidence that caffeine can help reduce the appearance of cellulite. Depending on your body scrub, it may be preferable to use it before your bath, rinsing it off in the shower before you get in. Opting for a moisturising bath oil will help smooth your skin further.

Once you are out of your bath make sure you moisturise. If, like me, you always forget to moisturise after a shower, then taking the time to actually use a body moisturiser after your spa bath is a must!

Hair mask

You could also treat yourself to a hair mask while having a soak in the bath. As before, you can rely on a shop-bought hair mask or you can make your own. A very simple one is mixing quarter of a cup of coconut milk with half a teaspoon of olive oil[28]. Simply comb through your hair and, if you have one, put on a shower cap (the warmth helps) and leave in for 20 minutes. Coconut milk and olive oil are good for moisturising and softening hair so a great option for dry hair. For slightly oilier hair, or hair that is looking a bit dull, mix a ripe avocado with

---

27   https://www.healthline.com/health/skin/diy-body-scrub#coffee-scrub

28   https://www.marieclaire.com/beauty/hair/a28285/homemade-hair-masks/

a tablespoon of apple vinegar, a tablespoon of oatmeal (or stick some oats in a blender) and a tablespoon of agave syrup, plus 2-3 drops of rosemary essential oil, if you have any (good for boosting the circulation in your hair). Mix in around two tablespoons of coconut yoghurt – enough to get the right consistency. Apply to towel-dried hair and leave for 20-30 minutes. You can actually use this one on your face too.

Relaxation zone

Part of what makes a spa day so relaxing is having the opportunity to fully relax. Be sure to find a suitable location where you won't be disturbed and get it set up for relaxation mode. Make sure it is a comfortable spot, adding in cushions and blankets or throws to make it as cosy as possible. Light some scented candles (see chapter 31 for the benefits of candles), put on some gentle background music, ensure you have a good supply of water and herbal tea, plus your choice of reading material, be that trashy magazines or a good novel, and, well, relax! Try and spend at least an hour there and if you find yourself nodding off, don't fight it, a little power nap will do wonders and at least you don't need to worry about anyone hearing your snoring like you might at a public spa!

Hydrate

Another nice touch is to make a jug of water with lots of lovely bits in it, like you see in spas. Things like sliced lemon, lime or orange. Or cucumber and mint. Add in some ice and have it to hand throughout your time "at the spa". It's also nice to have some herbal tea to hand as well. But if you are not a fan of herbal tea then it's absolutely fine to stick with a good old normal cup of tea – it's your spa after all!

Hopefully that has given you a few ideas to help you create a fantastic home spa day. It doesn't have to be a full day though – you might opt to have a spa afternoon before getting ready to go out for an evening. Or have a spa evening. You could even invite some friends round or, if you have children of the right age, you could make it a mother-daughter activity – my 13-year-old loved a recent foot spa and pedicure session we did together one Saturday ahead of an evening watching Netflix.

The Short Version

- A spa day is a popular self-care activity but you don't have to go out to a spa – you can recreate one at home.

- The fact that you are taking some time out to take care of yourself is a fantastic way to boost your self-worth and wellbeing.

- Choose a day, or half day, when you don't have any commitments and get everything you might need ready.

- Create a relaxing space with scented candles, cosy throws and warm blankets.

- Plan your time with activities such as a facial, foot spa, manicure, pedicure or bath.

- You can buy the products you need or choose to make your own, using the recipes in this chapter or finding your own online.

- Build in some time to just sit and relax, perhaps reading a book or listening to music.

Chapter 21
Find the "at least"

"At least it's not raining." Victoria Conway &
Emma Fear

The Why

At university, my best friend and I had this saying, "*at least it's not raining.*" It's something we would say when life was a bit shit. And if it was actually raining at the time, we would adopt a more sarcastic tone when saying it! In fact, I think we tended to say it more often when it was raining, in that slightly defeatist manner we adopted in our early 20s. But is a saying that has stuck with me and the sentiment behind it which, although we perhaps didn't fully appreciate this at the time, is that there is always a positive in life, no matter how impossible it may seem. I guess it is similar to saying, "*every cloud has a silver lining*", but I think our motto is perhaps wider in its interpretation. It's not about finding the good in a particular bad situation. It's more about just finding the good in anything – whilst one part of your life might be going down the toilet, take a look around you and see that it's not all bad, there is always an "at least" in life.

The How

So, when you are feeling down or things aren't going your way, give yourself the gift of stopping for a moment to think about what the "at least" is. It genuinely could just be that it's not raining, if that is the case. Or you could challenge yourself to be a bit more creative. Yes, you may have had a stressful day at work and be stuck in traffic so running late for pick-up, meaning your child will be the only one left at after-school club and you go down that rabbit hole of working mum guilt but try and interrupt your usual thought pattern to think of just one good thing. Perhaps it's that you get to listen to an extra 15 minutes of your audiobook or to sit and work through the work stuff before you get home so you can be fully present when you do finally get there. It can even be totally unrelated to the present situation. For example, at least it's Friday or at least there's a new episode of Bridgerton waiting for you when the kids go to bed.

All you need to remember is that there is always an "at least" in life – you just have to give yourself permission to find it.

The Short Version

- No matter how rubbish life may seem at times, try and find a positive.
- That positive can be as simple as, "at least it's not raining", or if it is, "at least I have an umbrella" and if you don't, then, "at least it's hair wash night" – and so on!

Chapter 22
Plan your day

"Give me six hours to chop down a tree and I will spend the first four sharpening the axe."
Abraham Lincoln

The Why

Have you ever sat down to start work in the morning and just not known where to start? Or been lying in bed at night worrying about how you are going to fit everything in? I used to do this a lot until I started getting better at planning my day. And not just in the morning but also the night before. This means that I know what I need to get done the next day and what my priorities are. It also means that I know what my first task of the day is so I can just get on with it – I don't need to spend ten minutes trying to work out what to do first.

Having a clear plan of action for the day means you feel

much more prepared to tackle it, especially if you have a seemingly impossible list of tasks to get done. Planning ahead also allows you to evaluate those tasks – how many of them are critical? Could any be scheduled for another day or delegated to someone else? As mentioned above, it also helps to prevent procrastination, particularly if you set out the order in which you are going to tackle those tasks or allocate times for each of them. Indecision of what task to do first is just a form of procrastination and a symptom of overwhelm. The best way to overcome overwhelm is to have a clear plan of action – applying an order of priority is a great way to start seeing the wood from the trees.

Planning ahead also allows you to be more effective in your time management. You can batch similar tasks together and schedule the more challenging tasks for the time of day you are at your best.

The How

The system I use for work is a very simple one. I have two lists – one with my "must dos" for the day and another for the "if I have time to dos", the latter not being critical for that particular day. This makes my to do list less overwhelming, as I can focus on the "must dos", rather than face a page-long list of things I "need" to do. The key to this is being super strict on what goes on the "must dos" list – it should only go on that list if it absolutely is something that is critical to be done that day. This can be quite challenging to begin with but is worth persevering with because it does make a huge difference to how overwhelmed you feel when looking at your to do list.

The second element of my system is to prioritise my lists. To do this, I simply add a number next to them in the order in which I am going to tackle them, starting at one for each of my two lists ie the first to-do on my "if I have time to dos" list starts at one, rather than following on from the "must dos" list, because it's important they are treated as two separate lists. This helps me in a couple of ways. Firstly, I don't waste time between each task trying to decide what to do next. Secondly, it stops me from avoiding the difficult tasks by skipping those in favour of the easy ones. And thirdly, taking the time to think about the priority of each task in the round, rather than as and when I finish a previous task, allows me to focus on what my priorities are, rather than adopting the "who is shouting loudest" approach.

I can then work through my "must dos" list and then, if I have time, move onto my "if I have time to dos" list, crossing off each one as I go. At the end of each workday, I review my lists for that day and move anything I didn't get done to the next day, deciding whether any on my "if I have time to dos" list need to be promoted to the "must dos" list. I try and do this before switching off from work so that I know I have a plan for the next day. This means I'm less likely to be sat there in the evening worrying about how much I have to do the next day.

Another advantage of having a "must dos" list is that it allows me to more aware of how much I have on my plate when others ask me to do something. If I already have quite a long list, I can better manage expectations in terms of delivery.

As with any system, there are always a few spanners that get thrown into the mix – the urgent task that comes and jumps to the top of the list. So, I do need to still be flexible and do often end up slotting extra tasks into my "must dos" list (and if, for example, I need to slot it in between my existing task 3 and task 4, I simply give it a priority of 3A rather than renumbering everything else!) And that's okay, so long as my "must dos" list is still manageable. If it is starting to look unmanageable then I know I need to look at ways to resolve that – perhaps enlisting some help or speaking to the person I am doing the work for to query its priority or timeframe. Ultimately, having the information to hand in terms of what I have on my plate that day allows me to quickly assess my capacity for taking on other tasks.

I do find that my "if I have time to dos" list often ends up having the same items on it for a few days. The kind of background tasks that I do need to get done but not urgently. So, rather than writing out the same list multiple times, I also have a "master" to do list where I record those sorts of items. This list I can then refer back to when I have some capacity and is also a good place to record those random requests or ideas I have of things to do when I have the time, rather than having a specific deadline.

So, my lists cover what I am going to do during my day but what is also important is to plan when I am going to do specific tasks and write this down. I have a diary that breaks down the day into half hour slots and this is really helpful for getting quite specific about what my day is going to look like. It might start at 6.30am with my morning routine (see chapter 32) for an hour, followed by getting ready for work and the children sorted for school. I'll then plan out my workday, using my lists as a guide. This is particularly useful when I have meetings scattered throughout the day as I match the task to the amount of time I have between meetings. Ideally, I will try and batch similar tasks together, so have dedicated times in the day when I will deal with emails and another for doing calls etc. I also put in my daily plan when I will finish work and set aside specific time in the evening for my "extra-curricular" activities, like writing this book!

Having my day structured in this way helps me to stay focused and does make me more productive. That's not to say that it always goes to plan! There are always those urgent things that come in unexpectedly or a task I thought I'd get done in half an hour, which ends up taking more like two hours. And some days I am just not "in the zone" and find myself reverting to a scattergun approach or adopting fire-fighting mode. And that's okay. I can't let myself get stressed about not sticking to my plan or not managing to tick off all my "must dos" – doing so just exacerbates the problem and will mean it takes me longer to get back on track. If I find my day going completely off-kilter, then I try and take a step back and reassess my "must dos" list and my plan and move things around. If I don't do this and let myself keep on running around like a headless chicken, I just end the day (much later than planned) exhausted and deflated. Taking a moment to stop and breathe enables me to recalibrate my day and end it on a more positive note (albeit perhaps still later than planned).

Now, you may have noticed that when talking about the above system it is focused on my work. I have to admit I am not so good at planning my days when I am not working ie Saturdays and Sundays. These tend to be much more fluid and I find it harder to plan what I am going to do beyond the usual family weekend routine of swimming lessons and other children-related activities. On the one hand, I think this is okay. It means I don't have the pressure a "must do" list may bring. It also means I have the freedom to be spontaneous in what I am doing. On the other hand, this often leaves me feeling unproductive because I don't feel like I have achieved the things I wanted to get done at the weekend. And I admit to being very good at wasting time while I decide what I am going to do next. It also means I can quite easily run around being busy and neglect to have any downtime.

So, I am going to make a concerted effort to have more of a plan for my weekends too. That way I can have a set list of things I would like to get done for myself and prioritise those, as best I can around the swim run and other such activities. I can also set aside a dedicated time for when I am going to have some downtime and read my book, do a jigsaw or just chill out in front of the TV. That way I will feel like I've had a productive, as well as relaxing, weekend, and not get to Sunday evening feeling like I've wasted most of it scrolling through Facebook or running around aimlessly and achieving what feels like nothing.

The crux of all the above is that it is *me* planning *my* day.

That's where the self-care comes in. I'm taking control of my time and what I do with it, meaning I am better equipped to be able to say no to other people or things that would derail my plans. This comes down, as it so often does, to giving ourselves permission to put our needs first. To recognise that our time is just as valuable as anyone else's. And the beauty of it is, that in doing so you will find that you create more time fors doing things for other people and, because you have taken care of your needs and priorities first, you won't feel resentful doing it either.

The Short Version

- Planning your day can help make you more productive, reduce the feeling of overwhelm, avoid procrastination and build in more time to do the things you want to do.

- Try planning your day the night before, writing out your to-do list before switching off for the evening.

- Split your to-do list into two – the first comprising the "must dos" for that day and the second setting out the less critical "if I have time to dos".

- Give your list an order of priority so you know the order in which you are going to tackle things.

- Don't beat yourself up if your day doesn't go to plan – just take a moment to reassess and go from there.

- Try planning your free time more, as well as your work time, to ensure you are getting the most out of that time too.

Chapter 23
Journal

"I never travel without my diary. One should always have something sensational to read on the train." Oscar Wilde

---

The Why

Recently, I found my old childhood diaries in the old wooden box I kept them locked away in, away from the prying eyes of my siblings. Flicking through them (I haven't been able to bring myself to read them too closely!), there is a lot of angst and drama, the focus switching between family and friendship woes and my latest crush. I remember though that writing in my diary was a kind of solace and reassuring, knowing that I always had "John" to talk to. John was a teddy bear I had when I was younger and when I first started writing my diary, at about 10 or 11, I started it "Dear John" (having no idea what a Dear John letter was at the time!) and it just stuck. However, in a way, it was a good approach, as it did genuinely feel like I was talking to a friend. As I got older my diary-writing became more sporadic and tended to only occur when things were tough. I remember when I went to work in Germany for six months whilst at university, I was absolutely heartbroken after a failed relationship, and I would write pages and pages of words in a Word document on my laptop. Thankfully that laptop, and the aforementioned Word document, are long gone, as I don't think I really want to revisit that time. It did though help get me through quite a sad and lonely time.

I stopped writing in a diary altogether in my early twenties. I'm not sure if that was because life got better or just busy! In the last year or so though I have started journaling. Not because my life has gotten worse or less busy, or because I don't have anyone to talk to, but more as a way to help get my thoughts straight and to gain clarity on some areas of my life. I don't do it every day but find it useful when I am trying to make a decision or when I'm feeling a bit crap about something. But when I do journal, I always feel much better afterwards – more clear-headed and motivated (they are often a bit of a pep talk!)

As it turns out, journaling is a great self-care tool, which brings with it a number of health benefits.

One of the main benefits of journaling is that it is a great way to help reduce feelings of stress and anxiety. Writing in a journal allows you to explore your emotions, release tension and fully integrate experiences into your mind. The technical term for this is "expressive writing" and it can be particularly effective when dealing with traumatic or highly emotional memories.[29]. It's thought that writing in this way reduces emotional inhibition, allowing you to better process difficult experiences. It may also lead to you being more open to seek support from others, having opened up about the issues that are worrying you. The act of expressive writing can also help you to better regulate your emotions and so increase your emotional intelligence, which in turn allows you to better interact and empathise with others. It can also be the circuit-breaker for the continuous thought-loop you can find yourself in when worrying about a particular situation. Writing it down forces you to focus your mind on one thing at a time and getting it all down on paper acts as a form of mental checklist – once you have written about that particular thought or feeling, you can mentally tick that off as having been considered. You can also use some of the more structured approaches to journaling, outlined below, to work through the particular concern

---

29   https://www.health.harvard.edu/healthbeat/writing-about-emotions-may-ease-stress-and-trauma

or worry, in order to reach a conclusion or decision, or make a plan of action.

Journaling has also been shown to help promote healing. One study in New Zealand found that people recovering from a biopsy healed faster if they wrote for 20 minutes about their feelings on upsetting events compared to those who just wrote about their daily activities. It was a very small study but other studies have also supported the idea that journaling can help recovery and healing, although it may be a result of the reduction in stress and anxiety referred to above.

The How

In terms of what you need to journal, at the basic level all that is required is a pen and some paper. You may though want to treat yourself to a new notebook specifically for your journal (who doesn't love an excuse to go to Paperchase?!) There are also specific journaling notebooks you can buy, which will often include prompts to help you with your writing. I would recommend avoiding a dated journal because that puts too much pressure on you to journal every day and makes it glaringly obvious if you miss a day (not to mention a waste of paper!) There is evidence to support putting pen to paper, rather than using an electronic method, as writing activates the reticular activating system, which is the region of the brain that filters and focuses information. However, I tend to use an electronic tool, mainly because my writing nowadays is terrible and I type much quicker than I write, but also because I'd prefer to keep it private and that's easier to do electronically. If you would prefer to type, rather than write, then you can simply use a Word document (which you can password protect if privacy is a concern). Or you can use something like 750words. com, which is what I tend to use. It's quite a simple tool that allows you to make a daily entry and, as the name suggests, encourages you to write 750 words. This is not a requirement though and I often write less. There are some fun stats too that analyse what you have written and show you what you were feeling and what you were most focused on, gauging your mindset while you were writing. It does cost $5 a month but there is a 30-day trial so you can give it a go before you commit.

What to write

There really are no set rules on what to write. You can just write about whatever comes into your head at the time; what you are thinking or feeling. And you can write as much or as little as you want, or that feels right, and as often as you want to or are able to. Don't worry about spelling or grammar (although admittedly correcting these is a slight force of habit on my part!) as you are not going to have anyone marking your journal entries! Try to make it legible though, as it can be interesting, and quite powerful, to read back through certain entries. But that's it, no other rules, you can just do whatever feels right. However, if you find the vagueness of those instructions challenging, particularly when first starting on your journaling journey, below are a few more structured approaches you could take.

Morning Pages

The term "Morning Pages" was coined by Julia Cameron in her book, "The Artist's Way", and more fully explained in her follow-up e-Book, "The Miracle of Morning Pages". The focus of Julia's work is to encourage creativity but even if you are not looking to be more creative, the practice of morning pages is still a good approach to journaling. The instructions are not much more complicated than my opening suggestions for approach. The task when completing your morning pages is to write in a stream of consciousness, writing about whatever comes into your head. This could be anything from worrying about whether you have enough milk for the kids' breakfast or ranting about the guy who stole your parking space yesterday, to a deeper exploration as to why you are so terrified of your upcoming presentation or writing about your dreams and desires for the future. There are a couple of rules though. First, you should write three pages of A4 or, if you are using a computer, 750 words, and no more. This word target, and limit, is designed to encourage you to delve deeper into your thoughts but not to get carried away and too self-involved. It can be challenging to write that much but this forces you to move on from the surface thoughts and to look more closely at some of the bigger things going on in your head. Some days will be more challenging than others but you will find that often, once you get going, hitting your page or word count comes quite easily.

The second rule is to not censor what you write, let it free flow and don't stop and think whether you should write about a particular thought or not. Often, if you are hesitating about whether you should write about it or not, it's a sign you really need to. This leads onto the third rule, which is make sure they are private. If you hold any fear that someone might read what you have written then you will self-censor what you write. This is easily done if using a computer as you can password protect your document or use 750words, as I describe above. If you are using a paper journal, ensure it is kept somewhere no-one will find it, even if that means locking it away. And if you are not able to do that, you can even destroy your pages once you have written them – even though it is nice to be able to refer back to them if you want to, more important is that you feel able to write without fear of them being read.

The final rule is that you should write these pages, as the name suggests, first thing in the morning. This is before daily life gets in the way, both in terms of making the time but also in terms of the thoughts in your head. We are often more relaxed and open to letting our thoughts flow when we first wake up. So even if it means getting up a little earlier to ensure you have some uninterrupted time, it is worth doing so. It is actually quite a nice way to start your day, carving out some you-time with your morning coffee and your journal. It is also a great way to have a bit of a brain-dump at the start of the day, to clear away the cobwebs in your brain, so you are ready to face the day ahead. It can be particularly useful when you have something to do that day that you are worried or scared about. Writing about how you are feeling about that thing, and why, can really help you get over that worry or fear, especially if, through your morning pages, you are able to come up with a solution or set yourself up with some coping mechanisms.

That does sound like quite a few rules, but the key thing is there are no rules about the actual content of your writing. And, as Julia herself says, "*there is no wrong way to do Morning Pages*".

Journal prompts

An alternative approach, and a slightly more structured one, is to use journaling prompts. As mentioned earlier, you can buy journals with prompts included and these can be really helpful, particularly when first starting out. Ideally, try and find one with several prompts each day and also some variation day to day, as that will help you explore different areas of your life and how you are feeling. You don't need a special journal though. A simple Google search for "journaling prompts" will bring up plenty of suggestions and I set out a few below to get you started. Try and have a list set aside ready for when you want to journal, rather than having to hit Google every time. This avoids you going down the inevitable Google rabbit hole and prevents you using the "need" to find the "right" journal prompt for that particular day as a means of procrastination or avoidance. You can even come up with your own, which has the benefit of being tailored to your specific set of circumstances and current challenges.

With each prompt, don't think too much before you start writing. It is not an exam question. You still want to maintain an element of a "stream of consciousness" referred to earlier, because you want your answers to be unfiltered. The prompts are more signposts for you to follow. And try not to skip any that you deem "too difficult" to answer that day – often those are the ones you need to answer most and tackling these more challenging questions is likely to have the biggest impact. If any really are too difficult to answer that day, make a mental note of the prompt and try and give it some thought throughout the day and come back to it the next day. You may find a day's contemplation of the question helps loosen the lips (or fingers in this case!)

Here are few prompts you might like to use.

1. How am I feeling today?
2. What am I worried about today? And why? What can I do to stop worrying about it? What will worrying about it achieve?
3. What am I grateful for today?
4. What do I absolutely have to get done today? What can wait until tomorrow?
5. Who is the real me?
6. What mistakes have I made? What can I learn from them?
7. What brings me joy in life? How can I do more of that?
8. What's the one thing I would like to change about my life? Why haven't I changed it yet?
9. Where do I see myself in a year's/five years'/ten years' time? Is this where I *want* to be or where I *think* I will be?

10. What are my top five bucket list items? How can I make these happen?

11. What am I procrastinating about? And why?

12. What's the best thing that happened to me today/yesterday?

13. What does my perfect day look like? How can I make every day more like my perfect day?

14. What do I want to be remembered for? Am I on course for that to happen? If not, how can I change that?

15. What is holding me back?

16. What are my past regrets?

17. How was I challenged today/yesterday?

18. What decisions am I avoiding making? Why? What decision will I make?

19. What does my future self look like? What do they do? How do they feel? How do they act?

20. What is my purpose in life? Am I living my life doing that purpose? If not, why not and how can I change that?

The W.R.I.T.E method

I came across this method when doing some research on journaling and I thought it was a good approach for those who like the idea of writing a stream of consciousness, as per the Morning Pages method, but needed some help getting started with that. The W.R.I.T.E method can be found on the Center for Journal Therapy website[30] and is effectively just five steps to follow when writing your journal, using the convenient acronym W.R.I.T.E. The five steps are as follows:

W – What do you want to write about? What's going on for you right now? How do you feel? What is currently on your mind? What is it that you want? Name it and write it down.

R – Review or **reflect** on your "what". Start by taking three deep breaths and then focus in on how you are feeling and then write it down. You should write how you feel or what you are thinking, right at this moment.

I – Investigate your thoughts and feelings. Just let your pen or typing fingers flow and explore the feelings and thoughts that came up in the previous step. If you are finding what to write difficult, take another pause and some deep breaths and let the thoughts and feelings come up again. Or try reading what you have already written and reflect on whether there is anything to add to that.

T – Time yourself. Write for between five and fifteen minutes and set yourself a target time for when you start.

---

30   https://journaltherapy.com/lets-journal/a-short-course-in-journal-writing/

You can even set a timer on your phone or other device.

E – Exit smart. This means taking a moment when you have finished writing to read what you have written and reflect on it as a whole. Write a few more sentences starting with phrases such as, "As I read this, I feel…", "I notice that…" or "I'm aware that…" Also, make a note of any action steps you have decided to take. This ensures you get the most out of each journaling experience.

The above approaches are just suggestions though. The most important thing is that you do what feels right. Feel free to experiment too. If you find that writing a stream of consciousness is too difficult to start with, try using some journal prompts. And then, once you get the hang of journaling, you can give the "go with the flow" approach another go. On the flipside, if you usually just start writing but one day the words aren't forthcoming, give one of the more structured approaches a try.

The Short Version

- Journaling has been shown as an excellent tool to help reduce anxiety, manage stress, increase your emotional intelligence and even to promote healing.

- It's easy to do – all you need is a pen and some paper or a computer.

- You can have a dedicated journal notebook or use Word or an online solution, such as 750words.com.

- There is no set way to journal and you should go with what works best for you. This could be a completely free-flow approach, or a slightly more structured approach using methods such as Morning Pages, journal prompts or the W.R.I.T.E. method.

- Ensure you are as honest as possible with yourself when journaling and avoid censoring what you write to get the full benefit.

Chapter 24

Cut down on the decision making

"Most of life's actions are within our reach, but decisions take willpower." **Robert McKee**

The Why

Although we may not actively notice it, we make hundreds of decisions every day. What time to get up, which mug to have our coffee in, whether to do some exercise or not and then which exercise class to do today, what to have for breakfast, what clothes to wear, what shoes to wear, what to tackle first on our to do list, what to have for lunch... You get the idea. And that's just the day-to-day stuff. Add on top of that the bigger stuff, like which school to send your child to, how much screen time to let your children have, whether you should change jobs, move house or where to go on holiday, and it's no wonder that sometimes even the simplest of decisions suddenly seems like an impossible task.

Making decisions uses up energy in our brains. Even the simplest of tasks, such as what to put on your toast for breakfast, uses up some of that energy. The more decisions you have to make, the more of that energy that gets used up and the harder it becomes to make a decision. And the more complex or serious the decision that has to be made, the more energy that is required to make it.

As with all forms of energy supply, the energy reserves used for decision-making are a finite supply. This has led to the idea of what has been coined "decision fatigue", which, although has limited scientific evidence to support it, certainly has a good body of anecdotal evidence to support it. Decision fatigue is when you have effectively used up the energy reserved for decision making after making a certain number of decisions, particularly more weighty decisions. Therefore, as making decisions uses up precious energy, cutting down on the number of decisions you need to make each day is a subtle, but effective, form of self-care. Reducing the number of decisions you have to make about the small stuff means you will have more decision-making power left for the bigger stuff. It is also closely linked to willpower, which is effectively the ability to make the right decision. When you are at the end of the long day of many micro- and macro-level decisions, making the decision to say no to opening that bottle of wine when you get home or whether to cook or get a take-away, becomes much harder. Have you ever started the day with all the right intentions and managed a healthy breakfast and lunch but then caved when it comes to dinner options? This may be decision-fatigue at play.

Likewise, have you found yourself simply unable to make a decision and so you avoid having to do so? This can lead to feelings of being stuck, so-called indecision inertia. You are fed-up with things being as they are but are just too exhausted to make the big decisions required to change it. So you don't make the decision and things stay exactly as they are.

The How

The good news is that you can boost your decision-making energy supplies, simply by reducing the number of decisions you make each day. And there are lots of ways you can cut down on your daily level of decision-making. A good place to start is by making decisions about your morning the night before, or even better, planning out your week on a Sunday evening. This includes things like what you are going to have for breakfast, what you are going to wear and what your first task of the workday is going to be (see chapter 21 on planning your day for some more tips on this). I recently tried planning out my entire week's meals, including snacks, in advance and not only did it mean I didn't stand in front of the fridge every lunchtime trying to decide what to eat, it also meant I wasn't so tempted to have extra snacks throughout the day.

Choosing what to wear each day is another easy win. My daughter recently asked me why she had to wear school uniform. And the answer I gave her included explaining to her the benefits of not having to decide what you are going to wear each day. I cited the infamous story about Steve Jobs and his "uniform" of jeans and a white t-shirt, explaining that the reason he wore the same outfit every day was because it was one less decision he needed to make. (This may not have been quite the answer she was looking for and certainly not one she agreed with!) So, try taking a leaf out of Steve Jobs' book (or even Barack Obama's or Mark Zuckerberg's books), and decide on a go-to style you can just pull on in the morning. I think it's worth noting here that it seems much easier for men to adopt a "uniform", be that jeans and a t-shirt or a navy suit and white shirt combo. I'm not quite sure why this is the case but I do know that I might struggle to wear the same thing day-in day-out. An approach that is probably more palatable is that taken by the likes of Grace Coddington (America Vogue's

Creative Director), who opts for a minimal uniform, namely mostly black with the occasional flash of colour. She has a few wardrobe essentials, including black and navy trousers, white shirts and black and navy jumpers, meaning she could easily put something together that works without having to put too much thought into it. So I think a staple wardrobe is the way forward.

There are lots of other ways you can cut out the more mundane/trivial decisions and the best way to do this is to keep a diary for a day or two noting all the decisions you make that day. Then reviewing this list and identifying those you could make ahead of time, adopt "default" positions for or turn into habits. For example, instead of waking up each morning and thinking about whether you will hit the gym or jump on the exercise bike, make it a habit to do that on certain days. That way, you don't have to "decide" to exercise that morning, if it's a Monday, Wednesday or Friday then that is simply what you do. Likewise, when shopping, make the decision ahead of time on what you are going to buy, write a list and stick to it. Be as specific as possible – include the brand or set the parameters eg buy the cheapest / healthiest / first one you see. If you have the choice over whether to walk to work or get the bus/train, set yourself the rule that you will always walk unless it is raining.

If you have an important decision to make then it is often easier to make that in the morning, rather than later at night, after a day of making other decisions. There is merit in the old adage of "sleeping on it". It doesn't mean you shouldn't think about it in the evening, use that time to list out the pros and cons or do some research. But hold off making the actual decision until the morning, when you can then review your pros and cons list and your research and make an informed decision. If a decision is time-pressured and you don't have the ability to sleep on it, try and take some time out to recharge your energy reserves before making the final decision, even if that's just a walk around the block or a few deep breaths in the toilets!

As with anything, there is a balance to be had here. There is evidence that mixing up your day and trying new things is beneficial too (see chapter 35). At the heart of self-care though is knowing yourself and what is best for you. If you are feeling overwhelmed or unable to make a decision, then try some of the tips in this chapter. But if not, and you are looking to boost your creativity, then try doing something new. And don't feel you have to stick to one or the other – being able to adapt your self-care activities dependent upon how you are feeling at any one time is another critical element of self-care.

The Short Version

- Our brains have a limited supply of energy for decision-making. This can lead to so-called "decision fatigue", when our energy reserves get depleted.

- Having to make too many decisions in a day or facing some tough decisions, can lead to decision fatigue.

- Look for ways to reduce the number of decisions you have to make each day. A great way to do this is by planning your day, from what to eat to what to wear.

- For big decisions, the mornings may be a better time to make these, when your decision-making energy levels are at their highest.

Chapter 25
Hold off on your morning cup of coffee

"Coffee was only a way of stealing time that should by rights belong to your slightly older self."
Terry Pratchett

The Why

I have never been a big coffee drinker but do like to make myself a latte each morning, as well as a couple of cups of tea. I'll then swap to decaf or herbal tea. It wasn't until recently though that I learnt that my morning latte was potentially impacting how well I slept at night.

Most people nowadays are aware of the need to reduce their level of caffeine intake, particularly after lunchtime, in order not to be kept awake at night. But what I don't think many people know is that it's better to wait until you have fully woken up naturally before grabbing that coffee.

The reason for this is that if you reach for that caffeine fix too soon after waking, your cortisol levels are at their peak. Cortisol is the hormone that is intrinsic in your sleep cycle and is responsible for making you feel more alert and focused. It also regulates your immune response system, metabolism and blood pressure. Cortisol is at its peak level around 30-45 minutes after rising and slowly decreases throughout the day, to encourage sleepiness in the evening[31]. It has therefore been suggested, that in order to get the best benefit from your

 morning latte, you should drink it mid-morning, when cortisol levels are lower. Even better is if you have been outside and seen some sunshine before you have your coffee. Getting outside in the morning sun (or overcast sky if you live in the UK!) helps your body clock stay in check and drinking caffeine before you've been outside can confuse your body clock due to the increase in cortisol.

At the start of the day, our body already has enough cortisol in its system from its natural morning peak. So, we really don't need another dose of cortisol from our early morning coffee. Elevated levels of cortisol over an extended period of time have been linked to an impaired immune system, high blood sugar and high cholesterol.

---

31   https://www.healthline.com/nutrition/best-time-to-drink-coffee

All good reasons for switching to decaf coffee at the start of the day.

The How

This doesn't really need much explanation – simply switch to decaf tea or coffee at the start of the day. Or opt for a herbal tea instead – remember though that green tea contains caffeine.

Decaf coffee has improved greatly over recent years and you can even get decaf coffee beans. Opt for a decaf coffee that uses the Swiss water process for decaffeination. This is a more environmentally friendly option and doesn't use the chemicals found in more traditional methods of decaffeination.

Try and hold off on a caffeinated drink until mid-morning, ideally after you have spent at least 20 minutes outside. And consider alternatives to your usual coffee. I have recently started having a Matcha latte in the morning, which is made from a type of green tea. Matcha tea contains caffeine but less than a cup of coffee (how much less depends on the type of coffee). It also contains an amino acid called l-theanine, which helps your body to absorb the caffeine more slowly, meaning the caffeine boost can last five to six hours. This in turn means you don't experience the same after-effects of caffeine consumption, such as a crash, anxiety and the shakes. Matcha tea has also been shown to have a number of other health benefits, thanks to its high levels of antioxidants, amino acids and other good stuff. These include increased mental clarity, improved focus, enhanced mood and lower cholesterol. To ensure its potential health benefits are maximised, opt for a non-dairy milk in your Matcha latte, as cow's milk can diminish the effects of those benefits.

And make sure you avoid caffeine after lunchtime so as not to impact both your ability to fall asleep in the evening, and the quality of your sleep.

The Short Version

- When we wake-up our cortisol levels are naturally at their highest.
- Caffeine increases our cortisol levels so is best avoided until our natural levels of cortisol have dropped.
- Try to hold off on your fully caffeinated tea or coffee until mid-morning, ideally after you have spent at least 20 minutes outside.
- Opt for decaf versions of your favourite drinks first thing in the morning, choosing the Swiss water filtered version if you go for decaf coffee.
- Try drinking Matcha tea instead of coffee for your mid-morning caffeine hit, for a calmer and longer-lasting caffeine boost.
- Avoid caffeine altogether after lunchtime.

Chapter 26

Give yourself a face massage

"Keep your face always toward the sunshine
– and the shadows will fall behind you." Walt
Whitman

The Why

We have long known the benefits (and joys) of a body massage, how it can relieve tension, increase flexibility and boost circulation. And the focus has always been on the back, shoulders, head and feet. The problem is that is very hard to give yourself a body massage – even a foot massage, while being physically possible, just isn't the same if you have to do it yourself! Over recent years though, facial massages, which you can do for yourself, have become increasingly popular.

While having similar benefits as a body massage, a facial massage has the added benefits of reducing puffiness, toning your facial muscles, boosting product absorption, releasing toxins, helping prevent wrinkles and giving your face a healthy glow. Massaging your face relieves tension in your facial muscles, meaning any wrinkles you have already appear less prominent and preventing further wrinkles from appearing (which appear when the muscles in your face are tense). It also improves the lymphatic drainage in your face, which allows the toxins to be cleared out. And the activation of the sympathetic nervous system caused by the massaging reduces stress. You can even use face massage to relieve sinus pain and headaches, by focusing on particular pressure points on your face.

The How

Although you can of course go and get a professional face massage, often as part of a facial, it's actually very easy to do yourself and just a few minutes a day can make all the difference. It's great to do in the morning, to bring a nice, radiant glow to your skin or, if you prefer (or have more time then), you can equally do this in the evening as part of your bedtime routine, as it's also very relaxing. You don't actually need any special tools, as just your hands will do, but you can also opt for a special face roller.

There are lots of videos and tutorials online showing you

how to do a face massage but I set out below the version I like to follow. This method only requires your hands but you can opt to use a jade face roller if you would prefer – if you keep it in the fridge then it can be a great way to wake up the skin in the morning!

Prepare your skin

Start off by making sure your skin is clean – simply follow your usual cleaning routine but stop before you get to your moisturiser.

Choose your product

When doing a facial massage, choose an oil or serum if you can, rather than your usual moisturiser, as they tend to allow more movement. Apply to your neck and face.

Start at the neck

Start by applying gentle pressure to your neck area to relieve any tension. Then use more gentle strokes down the side of the neck.

Next the collar bone

Move onto the collar bone and gently press down with your fingertips along the top of it, before using stroking movements down your neck and towards your collar bone.

Move onto your face

Start by cupping your face, leaning your chin on your hands for support and pressing down reasonably firmly with your hands. It feels a bit like giving your face a hug. Then start sliding your hands up your jawline, starting at the bottom of the chin and finishing when your palms reach your ears.

Next, run your fingers along the underneath of your cheekbones and then down the side your neck. This pushes any toxins down towards your lymph nodes for drainage. Then curl your forefingers and use them to apply pressure to each side of your nose.

Now, take your thumbs and press down either side of the top of your nose, just below your eyebrows. This is great for relieving any pressure in that area and can help reduce puffiness.

Finish with fluttering fingers

A nice way to finish a massage is to flutter your fingers across your entire face, gently tapping as you go. Take some deep breaths and you are good to go!

If you can, take your time with the above. Part of the enjoyment is having some time to just sit and breathe, rather than slapping on your moisturiser before rushing off to make packed lunches. If you really don't have time though, just spend a little longer than usual applying your moisturiser and give yourself a mini massage.

The Short Version

- Facial massages are one massage that you can do for yourself.

- They can bring many benefits, such as reducing puffiness, boosting product absorption, releasing toxins and helping prevent wrinkles.

- You just need your hands and some face oil or serum and you are good to go. Try following an online tutorial or follow the steps outlined above.

- For a super-quick version, just take a few extra moments applying your moisturiser with some care, rather than the slap-and-dash method.

Chapter 27
Use your best china

The Why

Do you have a set of china you only use when you have guests? Or just at Christmas or on other special occasions? We do – it's our wedding gift china – and it sits in its own special cupboard and, until recently, only came out when we had dinner parties or at Christmas. But then I read an article questioning why people saved the special china for special occasions or special guests. Were we not special enough to use the china ourselves? Was not every dinner shared with a loved one special? And it made a lot of sense. What message was it sending to our brains that we were not worthy of the nice china?

Now, don't get me wrong, we certainly do not use the nice china every day. With two kids and, more to the point, two boisterous dogs, the risk of breakage is too great. But we do use it more often than we used to. If my husband and I are having a nice dinner at the weekend just the two of us then we'll use it. And it does make the dinner feel slightly more special. We even use the nice cutlery too! At the end of the day, it comes down to believing we are worthy of spoiling ourselves by using the posh plates in the special cupboard and that goes to the heart of what self-care is all about. It's recognising that making an effort to treat ourselves is just as important, if not more important, than making an effort to treat others well. That may sound very selfish but it's not. It's all about ensuring you are at the top of your game so you have the capacity to look after others. It's about not thinking of yourself as not being worthy of the nice china. It's also about living in the now.

Life is short and making the most of every day is another element of self-care. Yes, using your china once or twice a year may well mean it lasts longer through less washing and fewer breakages. But would it not be better to enjoy the china today rather than have it sat in the cupboard until it is too late to enjoy it with the person you love?

The How

Another simple one – simply use the nice crockery more often and not just when you have guests. Make the effort to have a nice dinner with your partner, without the TV on in the background, and set the table nicely with the posh china. You could even break out the linen napkins! And if you don't have a partner to share a meal with, pick an evening when you won't be disturbed, make an extra special effort with what you are cooking for yourself and serve it on the posh plate you have hidden away.

And it doesn't stop at the fancy china. The same applies for all those other things you "save for best". The expensive dress that only comes out once a year, the nice bottle of wine your boss bought you last year that you're saving for a special celebration or the intricate recipe you saw in a magazine that you're waiting to try out when you have guests round. These are all things that you are worthy of having yourself. And every day should be a celebration – not just when you get a new job, move house or pass an exam. I'm not suggesting popping open the champagne every evening, just taking a moment to celebrate the small stuff as well as the big stuff. As the quote at the start of this chapter says, life is short so make the most of it.

The Short Version

- Don't feel you can only bring out the fine china when you have guests or for a special occasion. Recognise yourself as being worthy of the fine china and bring it out of hiding more often.
- Make an extra effort for a dinner à deux with your loved one or celebrate just being you if dining solo.
- Life is short so celebrate the small stuff, as well as the big stuff.

Chapter 28
Do a jigsaw

"There are no extra pieces in the universe. Everyone is here because he or she has a place to fill, and every piece must fit itself into the big jigsaw puzzle." Deepak Chopra

The Why

Every Christmas I get a new jigsaw, which I start on Boxing Day and gradually complete over the next few days and there is something very relaxing and therapeutic about my annual ritual. But despite how much I enjoy doing jigsaws, the only other time of the year I tend to do them is if I am on holiday and there is one where we are staying (although the deadline of departure day makes it slightly less relaxing towards the end of the holiday!) The reason being is that I get slightly addicted to it and can spend literally hours sat in front of my jigsaw, always wanting to just put in "one more piece"! And, if I am being honest, it feels like time-wasting, being sat there being so unproductive. But is it actually a waste of time?

Having learnt more about mindfulness (see chapter 36) and the benefits it brings, I have come to realise that doing jigsaws is a form of mindfulness. When doing a jigsaw, I am fully present, totally immersed in finding the right pieces and trying to fit them altogether. I'm so focused on the task at hand that I forget about all the other things I "should" be doing and stop worrying about work stuff or other stresses. That's why my Christmas jigsaw tradition feels so relaxing and therapeutic.

There are other benefits too. It is of course a break from being in front of a computer screen or scrolling through your phone. Jigsaws are also a great workout for your whole brain – your logical left-hand side and your creative and intuitive right-hand side. It's a great exercise in building your problem-solving muscle. Jigsaws are also said to help improve your short-term memory, as well as your visual-spatial reasoning. And the hit of dopamine you get each time you find two pieces that fit gives your mood a little lift. It has even been shown to increase your IQ! Researchers have found that spending 25 minutes a day solving puzzles can raise your IQ by 4 points[32].

---

32   https://www.newscientist.com/article/dn13786-simple-brain-exercise-can-boost-iq/#ixzz6uNFs6icC

And in our busy lives, it's something that can be picked up and put down very easily. My best purchase this year was a portable jigsaw mat – one that you can do your jigsaw on and then move it when you need the table you're using. The only risk with that is if I put it away completely then I forget about it. So I tend to leave it open but can move it to a different table if I need to. This means I can go spend five or ten minutes doing some of my jigsaw when I need a break or just some downtime.

So, I'm no longer treating jigsaw puzzles as my annual "treat" but as an act of self-care for when I need to switch off and escape.

The How

Jigsaws are easy to come by so there's no excuse really to not give it a go. Opt for one that is reasonably challenging, but not too challenging. This means you have to fully focus on what you are doing and you get a proper brain workout but it's not so impossible that you give up. Ideally, you will have a dedicated table space to work on your jigsaw, meaning you can come and go. As mentioned above, a portable jigsaw mat is a great alternative option to commandeering the kitchen table. If you are worried that once you start you won't be able to stop, set yourself a time limit. If you are sat there reading this saying you don't have the time to do jigsaws, I would challenge this if you look at your phone usage or social media scrolling. If the lure of your phone proves too great to pry you away from it, gamify your jigsawing – set yourself a challenge of putting in a set number of pieces each day. This will not only bring the benefits of engaging in a mindful activity each day but also bring a sense of accomplishment and achievement, which is a great mood-booster.

As for "how to do a jigsaw", well I'll leave that up to you – I'm not sure if there is any other way than sorting the edge pieces first, finding the corners, completing the edge and then filling in the middle. Next time though, to mix it up a bit, I may try starting from the middle and working my way outwards, purely to give my brain a new challenge and help build those neural pathways by doing something different! Admittedly, the thought of doing that fills me with dread, which is probably exactly why I should give it a go!

The Short Version

- Doing a jigsaw is a great mindfulness activity, as it requires you to fully immerse yourself in what you are doing.

- Jigsaws mean you are not on a screen and are an excellent workout for your whole brain.

- It has been shown that doing jigsaws can help boost your problem-solving abilities and improve your short-term memory.

Chapter 29

Take a break from social media

"Distracted from distraction by distraction." T. S. Elliot

The Why

If you are someone who frequently finds themselves lost down a social media rabbit hole then this tip is one for you. The average person spends nearly two and a half hours a day on social media, up by over 60% since 2012. That is an awful lot of time and whilst you may not think you spend that much time on social media, even if you spend just half of that time a day on it, that is still around 10% of your waking hours spent focusing on other people's lives, rather than living your own. If you find yourself saying you don't have time to read that book / work on that side project / do any exercise / spend quality time with the kids, just have a think about how much time you spend on social media in a week (or better still, if you have the feature on your phone, actually check how much time you spend on social media). Then ask yourself if you really don't have time.

As well as the amount of time lost, there are a whole host of other reasons why looking to cut down your social media usage is a good idea. It is difficult not to end up comparing yourself to others when using social media, leading to feelings of inadequacy or lack. And as much as you might be aware that the lives people portray on social media are through a rose-coloured filter, it is difficult not to have that feeling of envy of their immaculate white kitchen or their amazing-looking yet healthy lunch. Or the wonderful memories they are making for their children. And it's hard not to feel hurt if your latest selfie doesn't get as many likes as you had hoped. All these feelings can lead to increased stress, anxiety and depression, as well as giving our self-esteem a knock. Another aspect is the impact on our physical health. In chapter 16, I talked about the dangers of a sedentary lifestyle and I doubt many of us combine social media scrolling with any form of exercise. And if you are someone who likes to do a final social media check-in before going to sleep, this can have a negative impact on your sleep. The blue light from the screen suppresses melatonin, the hormone that induces sleep.

It also keeps your mind active and awake when it should be winding down.

Cutting down on social media can be hard though because it can become addictive. Each time you check your Instagram or Facebook feed you get a little hit of dopamine, the pleasure hormone. However, this is only a temporary thing so, as the effects wear off, your brain wants you to go back to the source of the dopamine hit and so the cycle begins again. This dopamine hit is even more prominent when you receive likes for one of your posts – the "like" acts as a reward, which then leads to the brain craving more likes. Social media companies capitalise on this and in fact design a lot of the features to increase the addictiveness of the app. One such feature, which was designed by Aza Raskin in 2006, is the "infinite" scroll, which allows users to keep scrolling without having to click anything to do so. This has led to users scrolling far longer than when some form of positive action was required to keep scrolling.

In light of all the above, it's a good idea to break the cycle and to take regular breaks from social media. It is also a good idea to limit the time you spend on it, ensuring you don't end up scrolling away hours of your day.

The How

There are various ways you can approach a social media break and the right approach for you will depend upon how much you currently use it and how much of a habit it has become. Here are some suggestions on how to cut down your social media usage.

Set time limits

The easiest approach to implement but the hardest one to stick to is to just say to yourself that you won't use social media at certain times or on certain days. For example, you may opt for a social media free Sunday, or tell yourself that you won't use it before 8am and after 8pm each day. This approach will work well if you have the willpower to stick to it and perhaps it is worth trying this to begin with and if it doesn't work you can try the next approach.

Use time limit / blocker apps

The alternative approach is to still set certain times and breaks for usage but to put in place mechanisms to support you in sticking to those time limits. Most phones will allow you to put time limits on your social media apps so using those can be helpful. And / or, if you use your computer to check social media, there are various web applications that can do the same thing, such as Cold Turkey Blocker. This means you will be prevented from accessing the apps and sites you set limits on during the times they are meant to be off-limits. You can of course always get round these sorts of blockers but they make it harder for you to access the sites, giving you the time to stop and think whether you really need to go onto the site.

Delete the app from your phone

I deleted the Facebook and Instagram apps from my phone a while ago, as I was finding they were becoming my "go-to" activities when I was bored, looking for a distraction or procrastinating. This is quite an extreme approach but can have the desired effect. It can be particularly useful to break the autopilot nature of social media usage. Like the previous approach, there are ways round it. I have found myself using the web-version of Facebook on my phone, which does defeat the purpose of deleting the app. Which leads me onto the next approach.

Change the habit cycle

Habits are a cycle of trigger – action (ie the habit) – reward. In the context of social media scrolling, there can be a number of triggers, mine being those mentioned above, such as boredom. When I am bored, I reach for my phone and go to Facebook and start scrolling – that is my action – and I am rewarded with that dopamine hit I talked about earlier. And that has become my habit.

To break that habit, I am looking at ways to replace the action of going to Facebook, with an alternative, more positive action. There are lots of actions I could replace it with, such as getting up and walking around the room or doing star jumps. Or picking up a book. The action I've opted for is one that still involves my phone, because it feels like a more gradual move. Now, each time I reach for my phone, I have told myself I have to go to my Gratitude app and add one thing that I am grateful for (see chapter 17 on the benefits of gratitude). So far, I am seeing mixed results – the biggest barrier is remembering to go to the Gratitude app rather than Facebook because doing the latter has become such an auto-pilot action I don't always realise I'm doing it until it's too late! But I am persevering with it and am hopeful that after a while I will have managed to break my Facebook habit. There are lots of books out there on habits and how to change them (James Clear's Atomic Habits being the Holy Grail in this area) so I would recommend reading around the subject to gain a better understanding on how to break your social media habit if you are finding it a difficult one to crack.

Hopefully one of the above approaches works for you and you start to feel the benefits of doing so. And of course the added bonus of taking a break from social media is that it frees up time, and headspace, to practise some of the other self-care tips in this book!

The Short Version

- The average person spends two and a half hours a day on social media, which is two and half hours they could be spending doing something more productive or beneficial to their health – or, even better, practising self-care!

- The inevitable comparison that takes place when seeing others' apparently amazing lives can lead to feelings of inadequacy.

- Cutting down on your social media use can be difficult to do, especially if it has become your go-to habit when you are bored or avoiding doing something else.

- You can try deleting the apps from your phone, setting yourself time limits or look at ways to break the habit cycle, substituting social media scrolling for a more positive habit.

Chapter 30
Give someone a hug

"A hug a day keeps the demons at bay." German proverb

The Why

I didn't really class myself as a "hugger". Don't get me wrong, I have always hugged people – my husband, my children and my friends and family to greet them and say goodbye. But it wasn't something I consciously recognised as needing. And then COVID hit and the hugs from friends I took for granted disappeared – literally overnight. And it wasn't really until a very good friend of mine gave me an illicit hug on a rainy Cornwall beach after I'd spent three nights camping during a storm and so was feeling downright miserable, did I realise quite how much I had missed those hugs.

And there is some science behind this. In fact, there is even a "cuddle hormone"! Oxytocin is a hormone that is associated with happiness and reduced stress, as well as nurturing, and our levels of this hormone increase when we hug someone. This has a particularly strong effect on women, resulting in a decrease in stress hormones, as well as in blood pressure. It does need to be a wanted hug but it doesn't have to be a human you are hugging – hugging your dog for example can also trigger the release of oxytocin. As an aside, it's also the hormone women release when breastfeeding, hence the nurturing feelings it invokes.

As another aside, oxytocin helps induce contractions during labour while at the same time helping to decrease our sensation to pain. And it's this lowering of tolerance to pain that supports the idea that hugs can help with pain relief. It's perhaps why our first instinct when our child falls over and hurts themselves is to give them a hug.

Hugging may also help protect you from illness, with one study[33] showing that those of us who have more

---

[33]   "Does Hugging Provide Stress-Buffering Social Support? A Study of Susceptibility to Upper Respiratory Infection and Illness.", Cohen S, Janicki-Deverts D, Turner RB, Doyle WJ., Psychological Science. 2015;26(2):135-147

hugs and social support suffered less severe symptoms from an illness. And it can even help with lowering our risk of heart disease, due to the oxytocin lowering blood pressure.

So, there is a lot of science to back up the importance of hugs. And it explains why so many of us struggled with the lack of hugs during social distancing.

The How

The self-care message here is to hug people, or pets, as much as you can. If you feel yourself starting to get stressed then go give someone a hug – ideally someone you know! Try and start each day giving someone you love a cuddle, be that your partner, your children or even your cat. Take that extra few minutes at bedtime to give your kids a cuddle. And if you are still feeling a little reticent about hugging people outside your family unit, there are a few things you can do to make hugging safer. This includes not hugging face-to-face, doing it outside and/or wearing a mask when hugging (who would have thought a couple of years ago that I'd be suggesting wearing a mask to hug someone!)

In terms of the physical action of hugging someone, I don't think I need to explain the how! Although there is actually a wikiHow page entitled "How to give good hugs"[34]! Apparently, the key first step is knowing when to give someone a hug, which does actually make sense, particularly as we come out of a pandemic – not everyone is comfortable with giving hugs yet. Another point in their step-by-step guide, which I think is also worth noting, is that it needs to be a genuine hug. There is nothing worse than a hug that feels awkward or forced but nothing better than a hug that feels genuinely warm, caring and reciprocated. Having read the three different methods set out in the wikiHow page, I would encourage you to give it a read, particularly if hugging does not come overly naturally to you – it does raise some interesting points on the etiquette of hugging.

---

34   https://www.wikihow.com/Give-Good-Hugs

The Short Version

- Most people appreciate the value of a good hug and there is scientific evidence to support the benefits of hugging.
- These include the release of oxytocin, a hormone that boosts happiness, reduces stress and relieves pain.
- Take the time to give a loved one or friend a hug to brighten up both of your days.

Chapter 31
Light a candle

"Man loves company – even if it is only that of a small burning candle." Georg C. Lichtenberg

The Why

Candles are an easy way to, literally, bring a little light into your life and they should not be the reserve of romantic dinners or birthday cakes. Because of their association with relaxation, lighting a candle can help you feel calmer and relaxed. Watching a flickering candle flame can be slightly mesmerising and so can temporarily draw your focus and attention away from the stresses in your life, helping to ease and soothe your mind. The soft glow from candlelight helps create a warmth in a room and can make it feel instantly cosier.

The key benefit of candles though is when you opt for

scented ones. These stimulate our sense of smell, which can invoke feelings of nostalgia and remind us of positive experiences, which in turn boosts our mood. Any whiff of coconut and I am instantly transported somewhere hot. And certain smells can help us to relax or promote other positive emotions. Lavender is a classic example of this, with its calming fragrance helping you to relax and promote restful sleep (just don't fall asleep without blowing out the candle first!) Citrus scents, such as lemon, lime and bergamot can be used for a more uplifting and energetic fragrance. And mint, rosemary and cinnamon can help improve your focus.

Incorporating lighting a candle into your evening routine can help signal to your brain that it is time to wind-down for sleep, particularly if you use it as a cue to turn off your technological devices which emit the dreaded blue light. Reading by candlelight in the evening can help you get a better night's sleep – just be sure not to fall asleep with the candle still burning.

The How

When choosing a candle, avoid ones that contain paraffin wax or artificial scents. Opt for 100% natural wax candles, such as soy or coconut oil-based candles. And choose ones that contain natural essential oils, rather than fragrance chemical oils. And always ensure the room is well-ventilated. There are some beautiful candles available nowadays, so choose one that appeals to you aesthetically or that has a scent you are drawn to.

Try lighting a candle and sitting for a few minutes watching the flame as it flickers and just breathe. It will help you feel instantly more relaxed. Or have a candlelit bath – a great way to relax before bedtime or to invite some romance into your evening. Match the fragrance to your mood or the activity you are doing. If you are looking to relax then lavender, orange or chamomile are good options. If you need to get focused on a piece of work you are doing, choose peppermint, rosemary or lemon. For a confidence boost on your Zoom meeting, try bergamot, sweet orange or sandalwood. And for getting you (and your partner) in the mood, try clary sage, ylang-ylang or rose.

The Short Version

- Burning candles can have a calming effect and add a feeling of cosiness to a room.
- Opt for natural waxes, such as soy or coconut oil-based waxes, with essential oils instead of artificial fragrances.
- Match your candle to your mood, for example choosing lavender candles for relaxation and citrus blends for a more uplifting scent.

Chapter 32
Try getting up early

"Wake up early everyday so that while others are still dreaming, you can make your dreams come true." Hal Elrod

---

The Why

In my younger years I was definitely not an early bird. My husband would probably say I am still not one. I have always loved a lie-in and while at university would be burning the midnight oil rather than dragging myself out of bed early to finish my essay or revise for an exam. And I am certainly not known for my early morning sunny disposition! Over the years though things have shifted slightly and, like most mums, the driving force behind that shift was the arrival of children. Gone were the weekend mornings spent lounging in bed and in came the crack of dawn wakeups and the occasional tag team of who got to have that extra hour in bed on a

Sunday. However, as the children got older and more capable of getting up and entertaining themselves, the lie-ins slowly crept back in.

Then a few years ago, in my continual search for more hours in the day, I came across the Hal Elrod book, The Miracle Morning. The book, which you may well have read yourself as it has become increasingly popular over the years, explains the benefits of getting up an hour earlier than usual and working through a morning routine, known as SAVERS. This acronym stands for Silence, Affirmations, Visualisations, Exercise, Reading and Scribing and the idea is that you work your way through these activities in the extra hour you gain from setting your alarm clock earlier.

I gave it a go and did find that I felt better for it, once I got over the shock of a 6am alarm call! It felt good to achieve something before everyone else surfaced and it really did set me up for the day. Admittedly, I haven't managed to make this a daily habit as yet and go through sporadic phases of nailing the morning routine for a while and then letting it slip for a few days due to some pressing work deadline or a late night out and then those days turn into weeks and months. But when I do get back on the early morning wagon, I do find it hugely beneficial. I no longer follow the SAVERS routine but instead have my own little routine that I work through, which I adjust depending on how much time I have in the morning. The one thing I find it helps with most is working on my personal goals, such as doing more exercise and writing this book! Those are my two current priorities and so I use my early mornings to focus on those before the hustle and bustle of daily life gets in the way. A lot of this book has been written while the rest of the house is still sleeping which not only gives me some peace and quiet to get on with it but also means I hit my word count target by the time I would normally be rolling out of bed. It takes the pressure off the rest of the day and means I am not trying to write after a long day at work when I've used up all my willpower reserves for the day and am just too tired to write anything vaguely sensible!

So why exactly is getting up early a form of self-care? Well, technically, it probably isn't. However, it is definitely a potential self-care facilitator, which is why I have included a chapter on it. Building in time to your day to do something for you, be that exercise, meditation, journaling or working on your personal goals, most definitely falls in the self-care camp. You might argue that having to get up early to practice self-care goes against the spirit of self-care – surely if it is that important you should make time for it without having it set the alarm early. My response to this is that the reality of a lot of our lives is often that it just doesn't feel like there is enough time to practice self-care. This is particularly true if you feel guilty about practising it. Adding in some extra time in the morning, which is not already ear-marked by the 57 other calls on your time, enables you to introduce some self-care into your daily routine. And once you start to see the benefits this self-care brings, you will hopefully come to recognise its importance and no longer feel it should be confined to the early morning slot.

You'll note though that I have entitled this chapter "try" getting up early. That's because getting up earlier is not for everyone and shouldn't come at the expense of not getting enough sleep. Studies have shown[35] that around one in four of us are natural early risers while another one in four of us are natural night owls. The rest of us don't really have a tendency towards one or the other. If you are a natural night owl then getting up early may not be for you. If you are not sure in which camp you fall, if any, then just give it a go and see how you feel.

The How

The quick answer to this is to set your alarm for an earlier time. But, for a lot of people, it's not quite that simple.

---

35 https://journals.plos.org/plosone/article?id=10.1371/journal.pone.0178782

If, like me, you have been a long-term fan of the snooze button, you'll know that that first alarm means nothing! There are various ways to tackle this. One way is to put your alarm on the other side of the room so you have to physically get out of bed to turn it off – once you are out of bed it is easier to stay out of it. Another is to take Mel Robbins' advice and jump out of bed as soon as the alarm sounds. Quit hitting snooze on your life and just get out of bed. The first time you do it will feel harsh but the more you do it the easier it becomes.

Setting your intention the night before can also help. So as you set your alarm visualise yourself getting out of bed as soon as it goes off. Another key mindset point is to not go to sleep thinking you are not going to get enough sleep because your alarm is set an hour earlier. Firstly, you should try and get to bed earlier to ensure you are not missing out on vital sleep. Secondly, if you think you are going to wake up tired then you will. Instead, think about how refreshed and full of energy you are going to feel when your alarm goes off and see if that makes a difference to how you feel when it does.

If that doesn't work and you are still debating with yourself whether you can have five more minutes under the duvet, try Mel Robbins' trick of using her five second rule. Simply count down from five as soon as the alarm goes off and when you get to one get out of bed. It sounds simple, and it is, but it does work because it interrupts your internal mind chatter and propels you into action.

Make sure you have a plan set out as to what you are going to do with your early start. If you are planning to exercise, have your exercise clothes ready to put on. If you are going to mediate, know where you are going to do that and, if using an app, make sure you select which session you are going to follow the night before. The idea being that you make it as easy as possible to get on with what you want to achieve in that time. If you don't have a plan then the temptation will be to lie in bed procrastinating about what you are going to do, which defeats the whole purpose.

You might find that it is in fact easier to get up early when you know you are doing so in order to do something you want to do. You are not getting up early to go to work, prepare the kids' lunches or to wash the kitchen floor. You are getting up early to give yourself some time for you, be that to go for a run, crack on with that side project you so desperately want to find the time to do or even just to take the time to sit and enjoy the peace and quiet with a cup of coffee. That is what you need to focus on when you go to bed – the thing that you are getting up for, not what comes after that. It's like when you are going on holiday, you have no problem at all getting up at the crack of dawn for something you are excited about.

Don't feel you have to go straight in for the whole hour earlier. Start by setting your alarm 15 minutes earlier and build it up in stages. And experiment until you find the right time for you. You might find that 30 minutes earlier is the max you can go without it negatively affecting the quality of your sleep. Or you may find that you are fine to build in even longer than an hour into your day.

To help with waking up earlier, try and go to bed earlier. Do you really need to stay up so late? Is your last couple of hours before bed meaningful? If you find that you are spending the last hour or two before bed sat in front of the TV or scrolling through social media, you could find heading to bed half an hour or so earlier will help massively with getting out of bed in the morning and will give you back some more productive hours in the day.

You may be wondering if you have to get up early every day or whether it could just be a weekday thing, for example. The correct answer is that it is better, from a sleep habits perspective, to have a consistent bedtime and waking up time. However, I find that quite difficult to achieve and will often end up going to bed later on a weekend. I find though that I do tend to still wake up early but have a greater temptation to go back to sleep if I feel I haven't had enough sleep. Like everything in life, I think moderation is key and sometimes you have to compromise, rather than going for the all or nothing approach. So my answer to that question is that it is up to you. You may feel better for sticking to it every day but don't let it become too much of a pressure point for you. If it does then you are more likely to revert back to your previous later start time.

The Short Version

- Getting up early can give you time to practise self-care, be that exercise, meditation, journaling, working on your personal goals or just watching the sunrise with a cup of coffee.

- Not everyone is a morning person though so don't force yourself to become one but do give it a try.

- Ensure you are not negatively impacting your sleep habits by going to bed earlier if you are able to.

- Have a plan for what you will do with your extra time to make the most of your early start.

- Go to bed with the right mindset of expecting to wake up refreshed and excited about your morning plans.

- Skip the snooze button and get out of bed as soon as the alarm goes off – try putting your alarm across the room or using Mel Robbin's five second rule to count your way down from five to lift off (out of bed)!

Chapter 33
Affirmations

"If you don't like the road you're walking, start paving another one." Dolly Parton

---

The Why

If the thought of using affirmations conjures up images of a hyped-up Tom Cruise, as Jerry Maguire, shouting "Show Me the Money" then please bear with me. The use of positive affirmations has been around for quite a while now and is a go-to technique in most self-help gurus' toolbox and are slowly losing their corny reputation.

Affirmations are basically positive statements that you say about yourself. They can cover anything, from saying how confident, intelligent, creative, successful or capable you are to specific traits and skills you would like to develop. If your immediate response is that it feels a bit weird to be talking to yourself in this way, stop and think about how much you already talk to yourself. And, more importantly, think about what you are actually saying to yourself. Chances are, your internal dialogue is mostly negative and critical of who you are and what you are doing.

And that negative self-talk is one of the key things positive affirmations are trying to combat. When we talk to ourselves in a negative way, for example telling ourselves we are going to flunk an exam, stumble over our words during a presentation or never amount to anything, we are at risk of making those thoughts a reality. We end up talking ourselves into the negative outcome – the more we convince ourselves that we are going to suck at something, the moret likely we actually will.

It makes sense then, that talking to ourselves in a positive manner can result in a more positive outcome. As we repeat our positive affirmations, we begin to reprogram our thought patterns and, eventually, the thoughts turn into beliefs. It's all to do with neuroplasticity, which is your brain's ability to change and adapt your thoughts and beliefs. There are whole books written on the subject of neuroplasticity but, in essence, your brain sometimes gets confused between reality and imagination. By repeating a positive affirmation, your brain begins to believe the statement is true and your behaviour begins to modify accordingly.

Various studies support the benefits positive affirmations are said to bring. These include reducing stress levels, improving self-esteem, helping with depression and increasing your self-worth.

The How

Firstly, you need to come up with what you want your positive affirmations to be. A quick search on Google will soon net you a whole host of suggestions. However, it is important to choose your affirmations carefully and to tailor them to you personally. A good first step is to identify the areas or situations in your life where you would like to see some change. It could be related to specific situations at home or at work or more general, such as improving your confidence or self-esteem. You could also focus on your desire to get fitter or lose weight or to overcome a bad habit.

Once you have identified the areas for change, think of a statement that describes the positive state you want to be in. For example, if you want to nail an upcoming client meeting, you might come up with a statement such as "I have all the knowledge and expertise I need to be fully calm, confident and poised in my meeting." You'll note that I used the present tense and that is important. You want your brain to believe that you are all those things, rather than implying that you want to become those things in the future. You will also note that the statement is realistic and achievable, if you assume that the meeting I am talking about is on a topic within my area of expertise. If the meeting is on a topic you are not familiar with and it is just not possible to gain enough knowledge in time to be credible in that meeting, then such an affirmation is not going to help. (An alternative one in that situation might be, "I am able to say no to meetings that do not sit within my job description without fear of recrimination.") That's not to say that your affirmations shouldn't be aspirational – I may think I am never going to feel that confident but if you can honestly answer the question, is what you are saying within the realms of possibility, then it is achievable. In fact, positive affirmations should be aspirational because they are describing the person we aspire to be.

If you are struggling to come up with a suitable positive affirmation, try flipping a negative one. Take note of your inner-talk and listen to what comes up. For example, do you hear yourself saying that you always give up on things and never get anything finished? If so, flip it around and turn it into a positive affirmation along the lines of, "I can finish any task or project I put my mind to and don't give up until it is done." Every time you hear your internal voice start muttering about always giving up, recite your positive affirmation three times. The more you do this, the less often you will hear those internal mutterings.

Below are answers to some questions you may have about how to use positive affirmations.

Do I need to write down my affirmations?

Yes. Writing them down allows you to craft exactly what you want to say and ensures consistency. It also means you will remember them and allows you to keep a record of your affirmations and to see how they evolve over time. Having them written down on a piece of paper that you can stick somewhere prominent also helps you to remember to actually say them.

Do I have to say them out loud?

No, you don't have to say them out loud, but they will be more effective if you do. Saying them in your head, especially when in a public place where saying them out loud will turn a few heads, is still beneficial because when you are talking positively to yourself, you can't be talking negatively. However, speaking your affirmations out loud has been shown to make them more effective. This is because when we say something out loud, auditory links are formed in our memory pathways, which help the thoughts to become embedded into our brains. This enables our thought patterns to change at a quicker rate than if we were simply to say our affirmations in our heads. You should also try and instil some emotion into your affirmations, as this will help your brain to forge the appropriate links. For example, if your affirmation relates to confidence, make sure you speak in a confident voice when reciting it.

How often should I say my affirmations?

Repetition is key to affirmations being effective so the answer is often – and regularly. Try saying them each morning and evening, perhaps linking them to when you are brushing your teeth (although not at the same time unless you want a toothpaste splattered mirror!) Or you could say them while putting on and taking off your make-up. Repeat each affirmation ten times, each time with feeling and meaning. You need to do this regularly so try and make it a daily habit. To begin with, you may need to set a reminder to say them each time. If you link them to a daily habit you already do this will make it easier, especially if you put the piece of paper with them written down on next to your toothbrush or make-up bag. Some people like to write them on post-it notes and stick them on the mirror.

A word of warning if your self-esteem is very low: studies have shown that using positive affirmations can be more of a hindrance than a help in this situation. This is because there is the potential for a conflict between your negative feelings and the positive state you are striving for through the use of affirmations. If you are suffering from very low self-esteem then do seek professional help before embarking on positive affirmations.

The Short Version

- Positive affirmations encourage us to talk positively to ourselves, breaking the negative monologue of our internal thoughts.
- Studies have shown that reciting positive affirmations can reduce stress levels, improve self-esteem and help with depression.
- Identify areas of your life you would like to change and come up with positive affirmations focused on those areas.
- Always write down your affirmations, use the present tense, ensure they are realistic but aspirational and recite them at least ten times each day, ideally out loud.

Chapter 34
Phone an old friend

"New friends may be poems but old friends are alphabets. Don't forget the alphabets because you will need them to read the poems." William Shakespeare

---

The Why

Do you have friends in your life that you have known since childhood or university that you class as good friends, or even your best friend, but you speak to once in a blue moon? And when I say "speak", I mean "text"? I have some very good friends who I have known for many years (some of these over 30 years to be precise) and we very rarely get in touch with each other and, even more rarely, see each other. But when we do speak to or see each other, it's never awkward and we just pick up where we left off. These are friends that all live at least two hours away, some even in another country, which explains the not seeing each other so often but, given the wonders of modern communications, not why we don't speak more often. Even with the surge in video calling we saw during lockdown, it took over a year for my best friend and I to get round to doing a Zoom call!

However, it has been shown that we are more likely to communicate regularly with people who live closer and see on a regular basis, than we are with those who live further afield, despite the digital age of communication we live in. It also seems that talking on the phone is fast dying out among the younger generation. The only people I tend to phone, rather than text or WhatsApp, are my mum and my grandma. Even in the work environment, the preferred method of communication for many of the team is Teams messages, rather than picking up the phone. We just don't seem to talk anymore. So why is this? And does it matter?

A study by the University of Texas[36] explored this and they found that people thought it would be more awkward to speak on the phone to an old friend, rather than texting or emailing. This was despite the fact that they believed they would feel more connected if they spoke to their friend. Through the experiments run by the University, it was found that the participants who were required to call, rather than email, their old friends,

---

36   https://www.sciencedaily.com/releases/2020/09/200911141713.htm

didn't experience the awkwardness they feared but did experience the connectedness they were looking for. And that's why picking up the phone is so important – it gives us that feeling of connectedness that, as humans, we all crave.

And it's that connectedness that makes phoning a friend a form of self-care. Belongness and love needs, such as close friendships, are third on the list of Maslow's Hierarchy of Needs, only being trumped by our needs for food and safety. While it's true that your need for love and belonging can be fulfilled by your family and the friends you see on a regular basis, there is still a need to connect with older friends you no longer see regularly due to geography. Often, these friends are those who knew you before you became a wife or a mother or any other label that defines you by your relationship to another. They know the you of your youth and have shared the ups and downs that come with that time in your life. And yes, you may well have both changed but it's those shared experiences that allow you to understand each other and reconnect so easily even after months or years of radio silence. It also gives you the opportunity to reminisce about those shared memories, something that has been shown to increase the feeling of belongingness and connectedness with others. Reminiscing has even been linked to making you physically warmer[37]! So a good chat about the "good old times" may warm more than just your soul.

The How

The short answer is of course, just pick up the phone! However, if it was that simple then I wouldn't need a chapter on this. Calling someone out of the blue you've not spoken to for months, or even years, is probably far too daunting nowadays. So, instead, why not drop them a message saying it would be great to catch-up and suggesting a call. And propose some suitable times – if not it will never happen as you'll fall into the abyss that is, "yes, we must speak soon!" And it is setting a time that can often be the stumbling block as you fall into the trap of thinking you don't have the time. But reframe it – if you were arranging to catch-up with a friend who lived locally, you'd arrange a time, date and location without too much trouble. Treat a phone call with a friend the same – give it the same priority as a physical catch-up. Put it in the diary or on the calendar so you block out the time – and remember to make the call!

---

37   Zhou X, Wildschut T, Sedikides C, Chen X, Vingerhoets AJ. Heartwarming memories: Nostalgia maintains physiological comfort. Emotion. 2012 Aug;12(4):678-84. doi: 10.1037/a0027236. Epub 2012 Mar 5. Erratum in: Emotion. 2012 Aug;12(4):700. PMID: 22390713. https://pubmed.ncbi.nlm.nih.gov/22390713/

And do think about using the likes of Zoom or Skype to do a video call rather than a phone call. Pre-lockdown I hated the idea of video calling but it has now become second nature, so much so that it seems strange doing a call at work without being able to see the person I'm talking to. Being on video also ensures you are giving the person you are talking to your full attention, and vice versa – there is no trying to surreptitiously unload the dishwasher or cook dinner when on video!

And don't make it just a one-time thing that you do as a result of reading this chapter. Set yourself the challenge of having a call with a friend you don't see once a month. Either with the same friend or with a different friend each month. Put a repeating appointment in your calendar – if it is with the same friend, send them the invite too. Yes, it may need to be rescheduled occasionally but having the appointment in your calendar means you are more likely to book in an alternative time rather than cancelling it completely.

The Short Version

- Talking on the phone rather than by text or email increases a feeling of connectedness.

- Reminiscing with an old friend can help improve feelings of belongingness as well as connectedness, both basic human needs.

- Instead of just texting an old friend, "how are things?", text them asking if they're free for a chat and suggest some times.

- Make catching up with old friends who do not live close by a regular date in your diary, just the way you arrange to meet up with new friends who live closer.

Chapter 35
Try something new

"If you do what you have always done, you'll get what you have always gotten." Tony Robbins

The Why

Do you ever fill stuck in a rut? Like you are just on the hamster wheel of life and can't get off? That's how I've been feeling this past week, dealing with the daily grind of life as a working mum. So, this morning I decided to get up, put on a new t-shirt I'd bought ages ago but not worn and, for once, a pair of trousers that were not jeans and go sit in Costa to work on my book. This may not sound like much but I came home feeling a lot better, the change of scenery and Sunday morning routine having helped me step off the hamster wheel for a couple of hours. Although I still feel like I need to do something more radical than going to sit in a coffee shop, like finally getting the tattoo I said I would get for my 40th, which is now over four years ago! Many of us spend most of our time doing things we've done before or variations of what we've done before – each having our own version of the eat, sleep, repeat cycle. And whilst there are definite benefits to some of our repetitive behaviours and habits (see chapter 24), there is a risk that we are living our entire lives on autopilot. Doing the same thing is the easy option. It doesn't require you to have to think too hard, to take a risk, to overcome a fear or stand out from the crowd. But, let's face it, it's pretty boring!

Doing something new doesn't just get you out of a rut. It has other benefits too, like making your weekends feel longer. David Eagleman, Ph.D, a neuroscientist who has studied extensively how our brains perceive time, says that when we are experiencing something new it seems to have lasted longer because we are having to focus more on what we are doing in order to commit unfamiliar information to memory[38]. That's why time felt like it passed more slowly when we were children. When we were younger, so much more of what we were doing and experiencing was new. As we get older, less and less of our daily lives are new experiences and so we

---

38   https://www.thecut.com/article/how-to-make-the-weekend-last-longer.html

can cruise through our days without paying too much attention to what we are doing. Interestingly, Eagleman also says that time won't feel like it is going more slowly when we are doing our new activity, because time really does fly when you are having fun! This is because when you are enjoying yourself you are not clock-watching like you might be when you are doing something less interesting. A good analogy used by Eagleman is that of a long-distance flight. It seems to take ages at the time because it is very monotonous but looking back it seems to have flown by (literally) because there was nothing novel about the experience (unless perhaps you got to fly business class for the first time, then it might be more exciting!)

It has even been said that those who seek out new things are happier and healthier – and even live longer! Pushing yourself out of your comfort zone allows you to feel a sense of accomplishment and pride, which in itself is a great mood-booster. It also helps improve your self-esteem (if you can jump out of a plane then you can do anything!) and improve your self-confidence – the first time you do something is always the hardest but then gets easier as your confidence grows (like public speaking). Learning new skills allows you to grow and opens up new opportunities.

And then there's this thing called "neuroplasticity",

which I have mentioned a few times in this book. Polish neuroscientist Jerzy Konorski first coined the term "neuroplasticity" back in 1948, although the concept has been around since the beginning of the last century[39]. The term (very basically) describes the way in which our neurons (brain cells) can form new connections and pathways, effectively leading to a change in how our brains are wired, as a result of our experiences. It effectively laughs in the face of the old phrase, "you can't teach an old dog new tricks". Improving our brains' neuroplasticity allows our brains to adapt and change, which in turn improves our brain fitness, cognitive abilities and ability to learn new things.

The How

Doing something new doesn't necessarily have to be something big like learning a language or how to play the guitar. It can be all those everyday actions you do on autopilot. Simply try switching it up so that you have to focus on what you are doing. Here are a few ideas to get you started:

1. Order something other than your usual latte at the coffee shop.
2. Try a different route home from work/school

---

39 https://positivepsychology.com/neuroplasticity/

drop-off. Select "shortest route" on your sat-nav or "avoid" the road you would usually go on.

3. Brush your teeth with your non-dominant hand.
4. Try a different supermarket for your weekly shop.
5. Try a new recipe for dinner.
6. Read a book from a genre you would not usually pick.
7. Go for a walk where you always turn left.
8. Work in a different room or location.
9. Challenge yourself to spend the day only eating foods of a certain colour (kids love this one – especially if that colour is anything but green!)
10. Listen to a different radio station.

Then of course there are the bigger things you can do. The sort of thing that you've thought about doing but haven't really had a good reason to, or the motivation to do so. Now you know the benefits doing something new can have, you have a good reason to finally start ticking off some of the things on your wish list. Again, here's a few pointers to get your brain thinking:

1. Learn a new language or how to say "hello" and "goodbye" in ten different languages.
2. Learn a musical instrument or join a choir.
3. Challenge yourself to visit a new tourist attraction once a month.
4. Take up a new sport, such as tennis, squash, rock

climbing, ice-skating or rowing.

5. Go to a painting/upholstery/calligraphy/woodworking/vehicle maintenance/cake decorating/candle making/photography course.

6. Go out dancing or join a salsa class.

7. Go get your make-up done at a beauty make-up counter.

8. Do a GCSE or A-level in a subject that interests you.

9. Go to an event you would not normally go to, such as the opera, ballet, theatre, live sports event or stand-up comedy show.

10. Redecorate a room in your house.

You'll note that I haven't included the big, bucket-list items, like travel the world or swim with dolphins. Doing the bigger-ticket things does of course count as "doing something new" but the risk with focusing solely on the big-ticket items is that you don't actually do them. For the purposes of this self-care activity, the important thing is to take action, so focusing, at least to begin with, on the easier wins means you are more likely to take action. And there is nothing stopping you from seeing this exercise as preparation for your bucket-list activity, for example, learning a language of the country you have always wanted to visit or taking a creative writing course to help you write that book you know you have in you.

The Short Version

- Whilst routines and habits have their benefits, trying something new has its benefits too.
- Doing something new can make your weekends feel longer, make you feel happier and healthier, and even help you to live longer!
- It can also boost your "neuroplasticity", your brain's ability to change and adapt.
- Try mixing up your day-to-day by choosing a different route home, trying out a new recipe or listening to a different radio station.
- And try taking up a new hobby, whether that's painting, cycling or photography.

Chapter 36
Mindfulness

---

*"It's not what you look at that matters, it's what
you see." Henry David Thoreau*

The Why

I have referred to mindfulness a few times in this book
and, if you've not come across it before, you may be
wondering what it is, and why I keep banging on about
it! Mindfulness, in its simplest form, is really just the act
of being mindful. But what does that mean? It means
paying more attention to the present moment. It means
turning off your mind's autopilot so you can live in the
now. We spend so much of our lives on a never-ending
merry-go-round of things running through our minds.
Things we need to remember to do. Things we wish we
could forget. Things we think we have to worry about.
Things we have to make a decision on. Mindfulness

allows us to step off that merry-go-round and catch our breath.

Being mindful involves noticing your thoughts and letting them pass. It involves noticing all the sights, sounds, smells and tastes around you. It allows you to give whatever you are doing at that moment in time your full attention. It allows you to appreciate the beautiful blossom on the tree on the way to work, instead of barely registering it as you mentally rehearse that difficult conversation you need to have with a client.

There are several benefits of mindfulness that people cite, some of which have scientific research to back them up. Some of the conditions for which mindfulness can be beneficial are stress, anxiety, depression, insomnia and high blood pressure. It is also great for general wellbeing and is a fantastic way to calm a busy mind.

It can help people become more aware of their thoughts and improve their self-awareness. Half the battle of challenging our negative thought patterns is being able to recognise when those thoughts are not serving us. Slowing down our minds and observing our thoughts allows us to look at them more rationally and carry out some quality control!

It also encourages us to enjoy the moment. Life flies by and all too often our minds are racing ahead to tomorrow or the next day and we miss fully enjoying today. Honing in on your current moment enables you to fully experience that moment.

The How

So now you know what mindfulness is and why it's good for you, but how do you actually do it? Well, the ability to practise mindfulness is something we all have within us. The hardest part is remembering to do it. To practise mindfulness you simply need to be present and to be aware of your thoughts. A simple way to start is to try eating mindfully. Not only does this enhance our wellbeing, it also helps slow down our eating, which aids digestion.

Eating mindfully means focusing on all the senses that are engaged when we eat. Focus on the smell of the food, its texture as you eat it and how it tastes. And you can extend your mindfulness to the whole ritual of preparing your food. For example, if you are having a slice of toast for breakfast, make the decision that you are going to focus solely on making your toast and eating it. Notice how soft the bread is before putting it in the toaster. Listen to the sound of the toaster engage and then feel the warmth radiating from the toaster. Take the opportunity to slow your breathing as you wait for your toast to pop. Notice any thoughts that pop into your head that are irrelevant to the task at hand. Acknowledge them but let them pass.

Once your toast pops, feel the heat of the toast and notice how the texture and colour has changed. Slowly spread your butter and focus on the sound of the knife scraping on the toast and see the butter slowly melt into the toast. Do the same with your chosen toast topper. Feel the weight of the knife as you cut it in two. Then sit down and take a moment to savour the smell of the buttered toast before taking a bite. When you do take a bite, notice how it feels and then how it tastes. Is it sweet? Salty? Focus on your chewing and then swallowing your mouthful.

As you can see, you can take any everyday activity and turn it into a mindfulness exercise. Try it while brushing your teeth, taking a shower or just making a cup of tea. The most important part is that you give your chosen activity your full attention.

What if I get distracted?

I can tell you now, it's not a case of "if" you get distracted. You will. Thoughts about remembering to pick up some milk later or the prep you need to do for your meeting will inevitably pop into your head, no matter how hard you try to stop them. The key is to not try and stop them. Notice them and let them pass. Think of them as clouds in a blue sky – the ones that look like they are moving. Let them float through your mind and then bring your attention back to what you are doing.

How do I get started?

In the words of the famous trainer brand, just do it! You don't need any fancy equipment or training. Just make the decision to give it a go. Start small, aiming for a few minutes each day. And then build it up. Try linking it to something you already do each day, such as cleaning your teeth, to help you remember. You could also set an alarm to prompt you although I find linking it to another activity works best because I often ignore an alarm if I am in the middle of doing something. There are also various apps that can help you build your mindfulness practice, such as Headspace, which is a popular one.

However you choose to practise mindfulness, enjoy the moment of peace you feel and hold onto that feeling to give you the momentum to keep doing it.

The Short Version

- Mindfulness, in its simplest form, is really just being mindful and allows us to step off the merry-go-round of thoughts that go round our head and catch our breath.

- It has numerous health and wellbeing benefits, such as reducing stress, anxiety, depression, insomnia and high blood pressure.

- It can also help boost self-awareness and reduce our negative self-talk.

- To practise mindfulness you simply need to be present and to be aware of your thoughts.

- As a starting point, try mindful eating, where you focus all your senses on preparing and eating your food.

- You can also try an app to help you get into the habit, such as Headspace.

Chapter 37

Plan something to look forward to

"Pleasure is found first in anticipation, later in memory." Gustave Flaubert

The Why

Before the pandemic hit, I had a list of things on the calendar I was looking forward to – or at least plans afoot to get such things on the calendar. Overdue meet-ups with long-distance friends, a family holiday, a weekend away with my husband for our anniversary, a day's cookery course and the usual get togethers with local friends that always brightened up what would otherwise be a rather dull weekend. And within the space of a few days, all those plans came to an abrupt end. And there didn't feel like there was much point making plans for the future because who knew when we would be let out to play again. None of these events were particularly momentous, I didn't have to postpone my wedding or miss out on a "big" birthday celebration, but having something to the look forward to, even if just a walk with a friend, has a significant positive impact on our lives. Remember how you felt when you were young on Christmas Eve or the night before a birthday (and maybe you still do!) – the build up to the big day was often more exciting than the actual day itself.

I have talked a lot about the benefits of mindfulness and how important it is to live in the present. However, there are also benefits to having something to look forward to. Thinking about a positive event in your future helps to balance out any negative thoughts you may have about what lies ahead for you – if you are worried about your job or having difficulties at home, being able to break the cycle of worrying about your future with thinking about a planned holiday or day out with friends can really help.

Gretchen Rubin, author of The Happiness Project and all-round happiness Guru, talks about[40] there being four stages to enjoying a happy event, (i) anticipation (looking forward to it), (ii) savouring (enjoying the moment – i.e. that mindfulness thing I keep banging on about), (iii) expression (sharing your pleasure with others, to heighten your experience) and (iv) reflection (looking

---

40   https://gretchenrubin.com/2007/08/a-key-to-happ-2/

back on happy times – who else loves the Memories feature on their phone's photo app?) Gretchen goes on to say that anticipation is a key stage because, by having something to look forward to, you bring happiness into your life before the event even takes place.

A good dose of anticipation can help motivate us to keep moving forward, even during the tough times, and give us a good boost of positive energy. It can break up what can sometimes feel like the monotony of the present. It has even been shown to help pathological gamblers hold out for larger-but-later rewards[41], which you may be able to relate to if you have ever saved for a holiday – the thought of sitting in the sun with a cocktail can be enough to dissuade you from buying that new pair of shoes that you really don't need!

The How

When it comes to planning something to look forward to, where a lot of us fall down (or maybe this is just me) is that we have all these great ideas and say to ourselves, "oh, it'd be great to visit [*insert name of country*]" or a favourite, "we really must get together". But we don't actually take action. My best friend from school and I live a few hours apart and we try to meet up at least

---

41   "Anticipation helps pathological gamblers hold out for larger-but-later rewards.", ScienceDaily, ScienceDaily, 5 June 2017

a couple of times a year. For years though we failed miserably at this because we would try and decide where to meet or what to do and never quite get round to organising it. Now though (well pre-pandemic), each time we see each other, we put a date in the diary for our next meet-up – we don't decide what we are going to do until nearer the time (we are both a bit last-minute on these sorts of things!) but having that date in the diary a few months ahead of time means we stick to it (unless there is a worldwide pandemic). So rather than get hung up on the detail, just get some dates booked in. Book the time off work for your holiday, even if you're not sure exactly where you want to go. Text that friend you've not seen for years and suggest some dates to meet up. Block out a day in the calendar for a family day out.

Once you have the date then you can work on the detail. And have fun working out the detail. Spend some time researching possible holiday destinations or checking out restaurant recommendations. My husband always laughs at me for buying a guidebook for each place we go on holiday – we have the internet after all. But the act of buying the guidebook, for me, is all part of the excitement of going on holiday. I love finding out about the local customs and how to say "hello" and "thank you" in the local language. That's maybe just my way of building up the anticipation of the holiday but the point is to revel in the anticipation, allow yourself to daydream about that cocktail on the beach or eating the local seafood.

Try putting a standing appointment in your calendar to do something fun. Yes, spontaneity is great and some might say a standing appointment makes it enforced fun. But the reality for many of us is that we are time-short and are guilty of letting the everyday get in the way of the someday. We will go to that new restaurant "someday" or take the children ice-skating "someday" or book that weekend away "someday". Having a standing appointment makes "someday" a reality. Try setting aside one Saturday or Sunday a month where you will have a family day out. Or the last Friday of the month as an evening out of the house. And see if the fun of actually doing something outweighs the lack of spontaneity.

Having things to look forward to doesn't just mean the big stuff though. Try building it into your everyday. Recognise some of your daily activities as something you look forward to. Whether it's a walk at lunchtime with the dog, watching an episode of your latest Netflix binge in the evening or your daily guilty pleasure of browsing the celeb gossip news sites! Seeing these types of activities in a positive light can help increase your happiness levels. You can take this one step further and start seeing them as "rewards" – a lunchtime walk being your reward for getting through a tough morning at work, your Netflix binge a reward for not raiding the fridge when you got home and your celeb stalking a reward for actually remembering to read with your child that evening.

So even if you don't have the resources to plan a big holiday or a night out at a fancy restaurant, you can always find something to look forward to. And why not kill two birds with one stone and plan one of the other self-care activities in this book, such as an at-home spa day, a bubble bath, breakfast out or a day snuggled up on the sofa reading a trashy novel – all things worth looking forward to!

The Short Version

- Although being present in the moment is an important part of self-care, having something to look forward to is also beneficial.

- Anticipating a future positive event can help bring happiness into your life and help balance out any negative thoughts or worries you may have about your future.

- Don't fall into the trap of talking about organising something fun to do, get a date booked in and then sort out the detail.

- Try putting standing appointments in your calendar for a family day out, night out with friends or dinner with your other half.

- As well as the bigger things, such as a holiday or a night out with friends, don't overlook the daily activities that bring you joy and that you look forward to.

Chapter 38
Do an act of kindness

*"Kindness is a language that the deaf can hear
and the blind can see." Mark Twain*

The Why

Most of us will have had someone let us out at a busy junction or perhaps had someone help us carry our pushchair up a few steps. Sometimes, these little acts of kindness simply bring a smile to our faces and a feeling of gratitude. At other times, they can mean the world to us, no matter how small they are. That time I was let out of a busy junction when I was running late to pick up my daughter from nursery after a horrendous day at work brought tears to my eyes, as did the time a stranger helped me put down my new pushchair to get it into the car after seeing me battling with it while my newborn screamed (seriously, you needed a degree in mechanical engineering to work out how to dismantle our pushchair!) And I remember how great it felt when a woman I didn't know told me she loved my haircut in the supermarket one time. The point is that a random act of kindness can simply brighten the recipient's day or maybe even save it. However, although a selfless act on the part of the giver, doing a random act of kindness has a positive impact on them too.

For many of us, the joy of Christmas is seeing the look of our loved ones when they open the gifts we have carefully chosen for them. As parents, the best thing about Christmas is seeing our children opening their presents (that's not to say I don't love receiving gifts too, in case my husband is reading this!) Part of the joy of entertaining is seeing your guest having a good time and enjoying the food you have prepared – it makes all the hours in the kitchen swearing at the pot of so-called pudding that won't set worthwhile.

Studies have found that performing acts of kindness boosts your wellbeing and levels of happiness[42]. One study[43] found that performing kindness activities for seven days increases happiness. In addition, they found

---

42   https://www.verywellmind.com/how-random-acts-of-kindness-can-boost-your-health-5105301

43   "A range of kindness activities boost happiness", Lee Rowland & Oliver Scott Curry (2019), The Journal of Social Psychology, 159:3, 340-343

the more acts of kindness the participants performed, the higher their levels of happiness. Performing acts of kindness increases our levels of "feel-good" hormones, serotonin, oxytocin and dopamine. It can also reduce our levels of the stress hormone, cortisol – as much as 23%, according to one study[44]. It has even been found to help you live longer[45]!

The How

Kindness does not have to be extravagant. Sometimes it's the little things that can make the biggest difference to a person's day. Sometimes these acts come naturally and are built into our fabric, such as giving up our seat for an elderly person or pregnant woman, holding the door for someone or letting someone pull out in front of you. At other times, more of a conscious effort is required to notice where an act of kindness would be appreciated. Be alive to opportunities to help someone or to offer a kind word. Even an understanding smile across the supermarket aisle to the mum of a screaming toddler can make all the difference. Make it your mission to do one random act of kindness each day.

---

44   "The impact of a new emotional self-management program on stress, emotions, heart rate variability, DHEA and cortisol.", McCraty R, Barrios-Choplin B, Rozman D, Atkinson M, Watkins AD., Integr Physiol Behav Sci. 1998;33(2):151-170

45   "Providing social support may be more beneficial than receiving it: results from a prospective study of mortality.", Brown SL, Nesse RM, Vinokur AD, Smith DM., Psychol Sci. 2003;14(4):320-327

There are lots of ideas on the internet for things to do but below are some to get you started:

1. Let at least one person pull out in front of you on your commute each day.
2. Give at least one person a compliment each day.
3. Text a friend saying how you are thinking of them.
4. Drop round some homemade cake to an elderly neighbour.
5. Pay for the coffee of the person next in line.
6. Send someone flowers for no reason.
7. Donate items to a homeless charity or do a Christmas shoebox.
8. Offer to babysit for a friend for free.
9. Buy a warm drink for a homeless person on the street.
10. Pick up some litter.
11. Recycle your old bras by donating them to women and girls in Africa (see for example https://yoursmallsappeal.org/)
12. Write a letter to an elderly relative.
13. Leave a larger than usual tip at a restaurant or café.
14. Buy your bartender a drink.
15. Put some money in the charity collection box.
16. Keep a spare umbrella in the office to lend a

colleague without one.

17. Write a positive online review of a local business.

18. Leave a love note for your other half.

19. Buy a "saw this and thought of you" gift for someone, just because.

20. Offer to take a photo of a couple or family on a day out.

And if you want to dedicate more time to being kind, explore volunteering opportunities, perhaps at your local homeless shelter, school, village hall, animal rescue or youth group. Or do a 10km run, a walking challenge or another fundraising activity to raise money for a charity that means something to you. You can also give blood or, for the more creative among us, knit hats for premature babies. The world is full of opportunities to do something kind, you just have to think to do it and you will feel so much better for doing so.

The Short Version

- Everyone has experienced the feeling of gratitude when they are on the receiving end of an act of kindness.
- Being the person to perform an act of kindness is also a great feeling and is scientifically proven to boost your wellbeing and happiness.
- Look for ways in your everyday life to spread a little kindness, from letting someone cross the road to buying a friend some flowers.
- You can also look for other opportunities to devote more time to doing something kind, such as volunteering for a local charitable organisation or participating in a fundraising activity for a charity.

Chapter 39

Write yourself a love letter

"Watch what you tell yourself, you're likely to believe it." Russ Kyle

The Why

Do you ever stop and listen to the voice in your head? For many people, especially women, it's often a running commentary passing judgment on every aspect of your life. Telling you how tired you look, how you messed up that presentation, how you really shouldn't wear those jeans, how you suck as a mum because you forgot odd socks day, how you always give up and so on and so forth…. A constant stream of negative feedback. Very rarely does it acknowledge a job well done or that, actually, you're looking pretty good today.

I recently read Mel Robbins' new book, "The High 5

Habit" and I confess to being a little sceptical about it – giving a high 5 seems very American! And the idea of giving yourself a high 5 in the mirror each morning sounded even more American! But while I haven't quite managed to get wholly on board with the daily high 5 habit, the sentiment behind it did strike a chord. We should be our own cheerleaders. If we can't cheer ourselves on then why should anyone else? And no matter how shit our day might be or the mistakes we have made, we are just doing the best we can. Yes, sometimes that is not good enough, but we are only human. So, we need to be kind to ourselves. Would you ever talk to your best friend the way you talk to yourself? If your friend told you about a mistake they made, would you berate them and tell them how stupid they are? Well, maybe, depending on the mistake, but you would also listen to the reasons for their actions or remind them that everyone makes mistakes – we are only human. And it is that kind of love and support that you would give a friend that you should be giving yourself. We are our own worst critic, which can be a good thing, but we need to balance that with being our own best cheerleader.

Positive self-talk can help build your confidence and self-esteem and have a more balanced view of a situation you are facing. It can also help you achieve your goals.

It can even bring about certain health benefits, such as improved immune function, reduced pain and better cardiovascular health[46].

The How

Positive self-talk does not come naturally to most of us. It takes effort. And practice. The first step is to take note of your inner voice and note when it is being negative. Then try flipping it around. So, if you are about to give a presentation and you catch your inner voice saying, "you are going to fluff your words and forget what you are saying", turn this around to "it's only natural to be nervous but you are well-prepared for this presentation and know the subject well." And if it doesn't go as well as you hoped and you hear yourself saying, "that was awful, you are such a failure", flip it around to say, "you were brave to stand up in front of that many people and you did your best."

You should also try making positive self-talk a conscious daily habit. You could try the High 5 Habit of giving yourself a high-five in the mirror each morning. Or challenge yourself to say three positive things about yourself each morning while brushing your teeth. The next step up is to create some positive affirmations you

---

46   https://www.healthline.com/health/positive-self-talk#benefits-of-self--talk

can recite each morning and there are plenty of books and online resources out there to help you come up with these.

The one thing I would like you to try though is writing yourself a letter. This may seem ridiculous but give it a go and see how you feel afterwards. Simply grab a pen and some paper, or open a blank Word document, and write yourself a letter. In this letter, list all the things you have achieved in your life so far, what you are good at and what is good about your life. You need to include at least five things for each of those topics – and the more the better. You can include anything you want to, provided it relates to you and is positive. If you find it difficult to think of anything, at the risk of being morbid, think about what someone who had to write your eulogy might write.

Once you have written it, keep it somewhere safe and re-read it at least once a month, to remind you of all you have achieved and that you are actually pretty awesome. Put a calendar reminder in so you don't forget – the first day of the month is a good day. And on those days where you feel like you can't get anything right, read your letter again and know that that day is just one of those days. And, on each of your monthly readings of your letter, add a postscript to include another achievement or positive statement about yourself – because no matter how hard the month may have been, there will be at least one thing that you did well, despite want your inner voice may have been telling you.

The Short Version

- Our inner voice can be our own worst critic but it's important they are also our own best cheerleader.

- Positive self-talk and being kind to yourself is a great way to boost your self-esteem and confidence.

- Recognise when you are talking negatively to yourself and flip what you are saying to a positive statement. The more you do this, the more natural positive self-talk will become.

- Write yourself a love letter, listing all your achievements, positive attributes and what is good about your life.

- Re-read this letter when you have a bad day and at least once a month. And update it once a month for a regular dose of positivity.

Chapter 40
Read a book

"Books are a uniquely portable magic." Stephen King

The Why

I love reading and getting lost in a good book but find myself restricting my reading material to non-fiction books unless I am on holiday. This is because I am not very good at putting a good book down and can easily find myself "wasting" an afternoon curled up on the sofa with my Kindle. And therein lies the problem – my view that doing that is a waste of my time. Taking time out to relax, doing something I love and that lets me focus on something other than whatever stresses and strains are currently dominating my mind, really cannot be a waste of time.

Reading is a fantastic self-care activity because it not only allows us to relax but also to be fully engaged and present in whatever book we are reading. Immersing yourself in a book stops your mind flip flopping from one task to another as it tells your brain to just focus on one thing – the story at hand. It has so many other benefits as well. A study by the University of Surrey[47] found that reading reduced stress levels by up to 68%, which makes reading a more effective stress-reliever than going on a walk or listening to music. The researchers found that after just six minutes of reading a book that we were interested in the participants' heart rates and muscle tension started to ease.

Another study[48] found that reading may delay the onset of developing Alzheimer's Disease. The study found that the adults who had intellectual hobbies between the ages of 20 and 60, such as reading, jigsawing or chess, are 2.5 times less likely to have Alzheimer's in their 70s. It's thought that intellectual activities, such as reading, help keep our brain cells healthier, which in turn are better

---

47   "Galaxy Stress Research", Lewis, D. (2009), Mindlab International, Sussex University

48   "Patients with Alzheimer's disease have reduced activities in midlife compared with healthy control-group members", Robert P. Friedland, Thomas Fritsch, Kathleen A. Smyth, Elisabeth Koss, Alan J. Lerner, Chien Hsiun Chen, Grace J. Petot, Sara M. Debanne, Proceedings of the National Academy of Sciences Mar 2001, 98 (6) 3440-3445

able to control or slow the Alzheimer's process. Other studies have shown that reading 20 minutes before bed can help you sleep better. It signals to your brain that it is time to slow down and is a much healthier habit than scrolling through your phone before going to sleep.

Due to the use of our imagination when reading, getting lost in another world created by a good book can also boost our creativity. If you are in a bit of a creative slump, try picking up a book and you may find it helps get your creative juices flowing again, as well as improving your communication and problem-solving skills. And the more you read, the more emphatic you may find yourself becoming. Getting engrossed in a character's storyline helps us to view life and situations from another viewpoint and can challenge certain assumptions and stereotypes we may have. This can be particularly true when a book has an unexpected twist and can be quite powerful. I once read a book involving a form of domestic abuse and the surprising ending did make me question whether I had certain stereotypes that I was not previously aware of. As well as helping us grow emotionally, reading can make us intellectually smarter. Anyone with school-aged children will have heard the importance of encouraging your child to read in order to increase your child's vocabulary but this isn't something that stops when you leave school. Continuing this habit in later years can help improve our communication skills, both verbal and written – especially if reading on a device, such as a Kindle, with a built-in thesaurus!

The How

This may seem obvious – you just pick up a book! But here are a few pointers to get the most out of reading.

Choose a book you will enjoy

I have started reading War and Peace about five times and have never got past the second chapter. It's one of those books though that I think I should read, along with various other "must read before you die classics". But actually, while they may be fantastically written, they are just not the sort of books I enjoy reading. And that's what we should be reading – books we enjoy. So don't feel embarrassed if your go-to book is some trashy romance, so-called chick-lit or a gruesome thriller. And if you can't get over the embarrassment of your fellow commuters or family members knowing your current book of choice is a Mills & Boon romance, get an e-Reader! Reading is all about escapism and getting lost in another world, so choose books that allow you to do that. If you do enjoy the classics though, that's okay too!

Try different genres

They say a change is as good as a holiday so don't be

afraid to try reading something a bit different. If you usually opt for romance, dip your toes into the world of thrillers or science-fiction. If you are of the belief that Mills & Boon is just for desperate housewives of a certain age, put aside your prejudices for a moment and give one a go – you might just surprise yourself! There is comfort in familiarity and sometimes it is the familiarity of your usual genre that is just the tonic you need. But mixing it up every now and again may open up a whole new literary world to you.

You don't have to finish every book

For a long time I struggled with this and admittedly still finish most books I start reading once I have got past the first few chapters – War and Peace being a notable exception! But reading a book you are not enjoying is not going to bring the same self-care benefits as one that is floating your boat. You are not going to be focused on it and it will feel more like a chore than a pleasure – just one more thing on your to-do list! Yes, you should give a book a chance to get going but if you are finding that it is becoming hard work then stop. You're no longer at school reading a set text, you are free to stop whenever you want to! If you have bought the paper version of the book and it feels like a waste to leave it half unread, give it to a friend who may enjoy it more than you or donate it to charity. This is harder to do with an eBook but perhaps you could write an honest review of the book – not scathing but perhaps pointing out who it might be more suitable for.

Have a reading day

One thing I struggle with is not being able to put a good book down, which is why I usually only read fiction on holiday. If not, I find myself reading too late in the evening and so am exhausted the next day. My way round this is to give myself a reading day. This is basically me giving myself permission to sit and read my book for the day (or maybe just the afternoon) and then lose myself in my book for a few hours. Another approach is to reach for a book rather than your phone when enjoying a weekend lie-in – grab a cup of tea and ease your way into the day with a few chapters.

Read on your "commute"

Years ago I had an hour's train commute each morning and evening, which would fly by with the help of a good book. Commuting is a great time to choose to read a book and much better for you than spending that time scrolling through social media. However, with the pandemic forcing many of us to work from home and likely to change the way we work in the future, our commuting time has been, and will most likely be, dramatically reduced. Does that mean we have to lose that reading time? It doesn't have to, especially if you don't get to stay in bed any longer thanks to children. You could choose to still have half an hour when you've finished work in the evening to read a few chapters of your book. You may find it helps you make the transition from work to home life.

Read or listen?

Audiobooks have increased hugely in popularity in recent years, with the likes of Audible allowing you to listen to a book rather than having to read it. But does it make any difference from a self-care perspective as to whether you are better off reading rather than listening to a book? There is not currently a great deal of evidence to be able to answer this one way or another and your choice of medium will be a personal one. You may prefer to have the book read by the author, meaning you are more likely to interpret the words as the author intended you to. Or you may prefer to let your imagination create its own interpretation of the story, as well as the character's voices. In terms of taking in information contained in a book, studies have shown little difference in information retention between the two formats. Again, it may also come down to personal preference – some people remember information better if they read it while others learn more when they listen to the information.

However, the one difference that I think does have the

potential to impact the self-care benefits of enjoying a good book is the ability to multi-task while listening to an Audible book. I am most definitely guilty of this one as I tend to only listen to an Audible book while driving, walking the dog or doing the housework. Whilst listening to a book makes certain tasks more enjoyable, such as doing the housework, it means that you are not benefitting from being fully immersed in your book. I certainly find my mind wandering more when I'm listening, rather than reading, a book. It also detracts from the other activity I am doing while listening to my book, such as walking the dog. From a self-care perspective, I would be much better off leaving the headphones at home and focusing on my surroundings while walking, taking in the changing colours of the trees and the sounds and scents of nature. So, if you do prefer the audio format, make sure the book is still your sole focus.

The right way to read in bed

Many people like to read in bed for a while before they go to sleep and, as mentioned above, this can help you get a good night's sleep. It's important thought not to read on an electronic device that emits any blue light. If you are using an eReader make sure it is one that doesn't emit a blue light or has a setting to turn the blue night mode off (often a "nighttime" or "sleep mode") or opt for a good old-fashioned paperback. What you read is also important, especially if, like me, you find it really hard to put down a book you are engrossed in. Try to pick something that is not too stimulating – a fast-paced thriller may not be the best choice. And be strict with your time limit – set yourself a maximum time or limit yourself to a certain number of chapters. I have a bedside light that gradually gets dimmer until it turns off completely which is a good signal that my time is up. Try to avoid setting an alarm though for your time limit as that is not very conducive to going to sleep.

Join a book club

Looking to combine your reading with some social interaction? Joining a book club is a great way to do just that. Not only do you get to share your thoughts on your latest book with others who have read it, a book club is a great excuse for a regular get together. You can either look for one in your local area or start one of your own. It might also expose you to books you wouldn't usually choose but that you find you enjoy. Be careful though that having to read the current book within the allotted time doesn't become a chore and yet another deadline you have to meet. Try and find one that meets as often as you are able to finish a book so you aren't putting yourself under too much pressure. On the flipside, having a deadline does mean you may well be forced to stop running around quite so much and sit and read. And if you like the idea of having someone else tell you what to read but are not so keen on having to meet and discuss your book, try an online book club. There are lots out there, including Reese's Book Club (led by Reese Witherspoon), Goodreads, Good Housekeeping Book Room and Ladies Lit Squad.

The Short Version

- Reading is a fantastic form of self-care as it helps you to relax as well as encouraging you to focus on a single task.

- Reading can also help improve your creativity and communication skills, as well reducing stress and may even delay the onset of Alzheimer's.

- Only read books you enjoy, not ones you feel you should read and don't be afraid to try different genres.

- Try reading before bed to help you sleep, use your commuting time (or the time you used to spend commuting) or set aside an afternoon to curl up with a good book.

- Consider joining a book club if you would like to combine reading with social interaction or are looking for suggestions on which books to read.

ABOUT THE AUTHOR

Emma Fear is a lawyer by day and, after finally getting round to writing her first book, "Guilt-Free Self-Care: It's Easier Than You Think!", an author by night (and early morning!) When not doing her day job, parenting or writing, Emma can be usually be found plotting out yet another new side project or sporadically picking up an existing one. She lives in Warwickshire with her very patient husband and two children.

Printed in Great Britain
by Amazon